Healing
the Soul *of a*
Woman Devotional

Healing
the Soul *of a*
Woman Devotional

90 Inspirations for Overcoming Your
Emotional Wounds

JOYCE MEYER

NEW YORK NASHVILLE

FaithWords
Hachette Book Group
1290 Avenue of the Americas, New York, NY 10104
faithwords.com
twitter.com/faithwords
First Edition: October 2019

FaithWords is a division of Hachette Book Group, Inc. The FaithWords name and logo are trademarks of Hachette Book Group, Inc.

The publisher is not responsible for websites (or their content) that are not owned by the publisher.

The Hachette Speakers Bureau provides a wide range of authors for speaking events. To find out more, go to www.hachettespeakersbureau.com or call (866) 376-6591.

ISBNs: 978-1-5460-3906-8 (hardcover), 978-1-5460-3851-1 (leather binding), 978-1-5460-3908-2 (ebook)

Printed in China

IM

10 9 8 7 6 5 4 3 2 1

CONTENTS

Contents vii

INTRODUCTION

When our arm is cut and bleeding, we can easily see that something is wrong and know what to do to take care of it. But when our soul is wounded, it is not uncommon for us not to know what the problem is or what to do to make it better. We may not even be aware there is a problem. Our inner life—our thoughts, emotions, attitudes, and willful choices—are all part of the soul, and when we have been wounded deeply through abuse of any kind, abandonment, rejection, bullying, and other negative experiences, our soul needs to be healed.

A girl whose parents have abused her will more than likely have fears, insecurities, anxiety, depression, or some other types of dysfunctional behavior. I was raised in an abusive, dysfunctional home and I had many problems in my soul because of it, but I was unaware of them. I behaved in the only way I knew to behave, not realizing that my behavior was colored by the abuse I had endured.

Relationships in particular were difficult for me, especially any kind of intimate relationship, because when anyone got very close to me they started realizing I had problems. When they tried to confront me about them, I became angry and sincerely thought they were the problem, not me.

I was very unhappy for a long time. Through receiving Jesus as my Savior, I finally—after many years of misery before and after becoming a Christian—began seeking Him for answers to my problems. As I write this devotional, it has been more than forty years since I asked God to heal my wounds. I pray that through this book I will be able to share some things that will help you in your own journey toward the healing of your soul. At the end of each devotional reading, I have provided a short statement that begins with the words *Declare this*. I hope you will take these declarations seriously because there is something very powerful that happens on the healing journey when you make commitments like the ones in this book and speak them out loud.

A healthy, well-functioning soul is available for every person, but those who have been wounded will need to be patient and steadfast as the Holy Spirit leads them through their own personal journey of healing. If you are one of the wounded, there are many things you will need to learn, so let's get started and get moving toward wholeness. Let's begin with a prayer:

> *Father, in Jesus' name, I ask You to heal my wounded soul. I want to be and do all that You want for me. I have a great deal to learn and I ask You to teach me and help me face truth in every area in which my thinking is wrong. I commit my life entirely to You and choose to open my heart to You in every area of my past. Help me and strengthen me through the power of the Holy Spirit, and empower me to have a Spirit-filled personality. Amen!*

> *May He grant you out of the rich treasury of His glory to be strengthened and reinforced with mighty power in the inner man by the [Holy] Spirit [Himself indwelling your innermost being and personality].*

> Ephesians 3:16 AMPC

1

Healing for the Brokenhearted

He heals the brokenhearted and binds up their wounds.

Psalm 147:3

Those who are brokenhearted are broken in their personality. They are unable to function properly because of their wounds. They have been deeply hurt and are unable to move beyond their past pain.

It is important that we don't merely park at the point of our pain and remain there for the rest of our lives. God is the author of new beginnings, and whether we are wounded due our own sin, or because of the sin of others who have harmed us, we are the only ones who can decide whether to move on or stay parked. Take your life out of park and start moving forward toward the great future God has arranged for you.

The apostle Paul is a great example of someone who kept shaking off the past and pressing forward. He moved past his own sin, past the persecution he received from others as his reward for simply trying to help them, past unfair imprisonment, beatings, abandonment, and many other painful things. He also moved past his own imperfections in his daily walk with God and said that letting go of what was behind was his determined purpose in life.

When we are hurting, moving forward isn't always easy because our mind and emotions are telling us to just give up. Although change isn't easy and is often painful, we have only two choices—to endure the pain of change or to endure the pain of never changing. It is easy to see which choice makes the most sense. If there will be pain either way, why not choose the pain of progress?

To keep going forward in the midst of personal pain takes a lot of courage. You may not even want to get out of bed in the morning, let alone be active and do what life requires that day, but if you live by wise choices rather than by your feelings, you can do it.

I vividly remember my father repeatedly telling me, "You will never amount to anything," but with God's help, I overcame his negative words. If those who should have affirmed you tore you down with their words, you too can overcome their words by seeing what God says about you and meditating on His words instead. God says many wonderful things about you, things such as: You are fearfully and wonderfully made (Ps. 139:14). You are loved unconditionally (Jer. 31:3) and accepted (John 6:37). You are precious and honored in His sight (Isa. 43:4). His Word includes many similar truths that will build you up and renew your mind so you can think about yourself and your life the way God wants you to.

Don't settle for less than the best life that God wants to give you. Perhaps you are facing a time of testing in your life right now, and the temptation to quit and give up is strong. Know this: You have what it takes to go through it and experience victory on the other side.

It's not too late! I'm sure the devil has told you the lie that it is too late for you. However, it is never too late for God to heal and restore anyone who truly wants Him to.

Declare this:

God is healing my broken heart and making me whole.

2

Do You Need an Upgrade?

But, as it is written, "What no eye has seen, nor ear heard, nor the heart of man imagined, what God has prepared for those who love him."

1 Corinthians 2:9

We rush to get every new upgrade available for our computer and phone. We spend money, wait in lines, do whatever it takes to have the newest and best. We are very aggressive about having the best equipment available, but are we as aggressive about having the upgraded life Jesus offers us?

The Bible says that the path of the righteous gets brighter and brighter every day (Prov. 4:18). This means God is always drawing us toward better and better things. He continually offers upgrades, and we should be determined to have each one of them.

Living the best life God has for you will require some effort on your part. You will need to educate yourself on the life He offers and what it truly means to be born again. As a child of God, you have an inheritance and you have certain rights and privileges, but if you don't know about them, you will never enjoy them. We educate ourselves through Bible study, reading good books about biblical principles, spending time with God, and being in community with other people who are seeking God as we are. We also need a lot of patience because God is usually not in a hurry. He is always working in our lives, but we are not always aware of it.

Simply going to church once a week doesn't necessarily help you attain the upgraded life you desire. It helps, but you will have to also seek God diligently every day of your life, not just once or twice a week. God has provided countless tools for us to help us grow, but we must avail ourselves of them. I want to challenge you to set aside at least 45 minutes to an hour a day and call it your "God Time." Make it a goal, and if you need to begin with less time, that is okay because gradually you will desire more. During that time you can study your Bible, talk to God in prayer, listen to a Bible teaching, read a book that will help you understand the Bible better, or simply sit in God's presence and receive His love.

If you do this diligently, you will find over time that you have changed and are enjoying yourself and your life much more than ever before. Any good relationship requires time, and your relationship with God is no different. God has so many wonderful things in His plan for you, and during this time you will learn what they are and how to access them. You can't use what you don't know you have! For example, you have a Helper, who is the Holy Spirit, and He is with you all the time. Anytime you need help with anything, all you need to do is ask. This and many other wonderful things are yours in Christ, so get busy learning about them and start enjoying the upgraded life Jesus died for you to have.

Declare this:

God has many good things planned for me, and I am determined not to miss any of them.

3

A Place of Mystery

He restores my soul. He leads me in paths of righteousness for his name's sake.

Psalm 23:3

I think it is safe to say that the soul is a place of mystery. We cannot see our soul, but we can and do feel its impact on our lives. All kinds of feelings, attitudes, thoughts, imaginings, and desires fill the soul, and they are often in conflict with one another. We may feel that we want to do one thing, yet think we are not able to do it. We have many feelings we don't understand or even know where they came from. Why, for example, would a woman feel intimidated when another woman she doesn't even know walks into a room? Or why would a woman lack confidence even though she is very talented? What causes insecurity, fear of failure, abandonment, or rejection?

These problems are definitely caused by something, and we need to know what it is. There could be multiple reasons we react the way we do in specific circumstances, but we will never understand ourselves if we continue to ignore and hide from the negative feelings and strange behaviors we have. Most of them come from some emotional injury we have sustained in our lifetime that has never been healed. It is impossible to go through life and never be hurt, but whether we heal or stay wounded is up to us.

It is easy to hide from our pain and live under layers of false identities in an effort to hide the person we really are, but it takes courage to find your true self and learn to live the life you were meant to live. Have you ever thought, "I just don't understand myself"? "What is wrong with me?" "Who am I, and what is my purpose in life?"

The way to find the answers to these questions is to look into God's Word. In His Word, we find His plan for us and we recognize the lies we have believed, perhaps our entire life, that have been used to derail our destiny and leave us confused about our identity. I believed I would always have a second-rate life because my father sexually abused me, but in God's Word, I found out that He could take my pain and actually make it work out for my good if I would let Him.

If you have been hurt and have a wounded soul, don't be afraid to open your entire being to God and ask Him to heal you. Remember, healing requires facing a lot of things you may have been ignoring or hiding from for a long time. It may be a frightening thought to let the light into your darkness, but I promise that you will be glad you did.

Declare this:

I refuse to live in the dark any longer. I will take God's hand and walk into the light and face the truth that will set me free.

4

A New Way to Live

Therefore, brothers, since we have confidence to enter the holy places by the blood of Jesus, by the new and living way…

Hebrews 10:19–20

When you become a Christian by receiving Jesus as your Savior, He actually comes to live inside you by His Spirit, and you can be led by His Spirit throughout your life. You no longer have to feel you must follow religious rules and regulations, thinking you can please God by doing everything "right." The Holy Spirit will guide you into God's plans for your life, which are better than anything you could plan for yourself. This is truly a new way of living—a way of love, peace, freedom, fulfillment, and joy. You can begin it today, and it is a journey you will be on for the rest of your life.

Anytime you try to do anything new, you have to learn how to do it. That's also true with a new way of living. Some of what you learn may seem unusual because it is different than anything you have done before and it is the complete opposite of what the world teaches us. For example, in God's new way of living, people who try to be first end up last, while those who put themselves last end up first (Matt. 20:16). If someone wants one thing from us, we can give them even more (Matt. 5:40). Instead of holding grudges against people who have hurt us, we forgive them (Matt. 18:21–22).

Jesus' teaching to forgive those who use, abuse, or wound us—and then to go even further and actually love and bless them (Luke 6:27–28)—was a difficult one for me. It meant forgiving my father for sexually abusing me and forgiving my mother, who knew about it and ignored it, choosing instead to treat me as though I were the one doing something wrong. Forgiving them seemed totally unreasonable to me. It took a long time for me to be willing to do that. When I finally did, it set me free and I urge you to forgive anyone that you have anything against.

Learning to forgive is only one of many lessons God has taught me about His way of living, which is why I say it is a lifetime journey. I am still learning. I want you to know that every path the Holy Spirit has led me to take on this new way has always brought me to a better place than I was before. God will never ask us to do anything difficult unless it will lead us to a better life.

Because the new way is not always easy, you may be tempted at times to fall back into your old ways. But if you will resist that temptation and ask God to help you persist in the new way of living, it will make your life better and ultimately easier than you ever thought possible.

Declare this:

I choose to turn from my old ways and let the Holy Spirit lead me in a new and living way.

5

The Goal of a Healthy Soul

*Beloved, I pray that you may prosper in all things and be
in health, just as your soul prospers.*

3 John 2 NKJV

Most women I know set and meet goals each day, such as "Buy the
groceries. Do the laundry. Take the kids to school. Pick up Mom's
prescription. Get Mary's birthday present." We also set goals for
each week and each year, such as getting to church every Sun-
day or going on a summer vacation. But how many women have
this goal: "Work on getting my soul healthy"? It's one of the most
important of all.

A healthy soul is a soul at peace and at rest. It isn't upset,
worried, angry, ashamed, or fearful. It is strong and steady, full
of love, joy, hope, compassion toward others, and confidence in
God. It can handle the ups and downs of life appropriately and go
through everyday life with ease.

As you read the description of a healthy soul, you may think,
*Oh, that sounds so nice! I would love that, but I just don't think it's
possible because I am dealing with [fill in the blank].* When you fill
in the blank, you may say "aging parents," or "difficult teenagers,"

or "a serious health condition," or "job loss," or "an abusive relationship," or "losing my friends," or "problems in my marriage," or "financial trouble," or "unreasonable stress at work." There are all kinds of situations that will cause you to think you really cannot have a healthy soul. They may mean you have to work hard to improve the health of your soul, but they don't prohibit it. Actually, the fact that you are going through these things is not a hindrance to a healthy soul; it's the reason you need one! The healthier your soul is, the stronger you will be and the better you will be able to handle your most challenging circumstances.

Just like you, I am no stranger to stress, but I have learned that things that upset us *will* happen. We don't have control over that, but because God has given us the fruit of self-control (Gal. 5:22–23) and because we can ask Him to help us, we do have control over the way we respond to them. I can guarantee you, based on personal experience, that it's much better to face challenges with a healthy soul than with a weak or wounded one.

A healthy soul is a worthy goal for all of us. I understand that in many ways it's easier to get the groceries or drop off the kids at school than to work on becoming healthy in your mind, will, and emotions. I also know it's one of the best things you will ever do for yourself and that God will help you do it. It may seem difficult to you, but all things are possible with Him!

Declare this:

I am determined, with God's help, to have a healthy soul, and I am committed to do what it takes to get one.

6

Overcoming the Accuser

And I heard a loud voice in heaven, saying, "Now the salvation and the power and the kingdom of our God and the authority of his Christ have come, for the accuser of our brothers has been thrown down, who accuses them day and night before our God. And they have conquered him by the blood of the Lamb and by the word of their testimony, for they loved not their lives even unto death."

Revelation 12:10–11

Sometimes the devil complicates the healing process because he bombards your mind with negative thoughts and accusations. He will whisper to your mind accusations such as, "You are so wounded you can never be healed." Or, "You aren't worth having a better life than you have right now." Or, "You deserve the pain you're going through." The devil is a liar, and he wants you to feel guilty and condemned. He can put thoughts in your mind, but that doesn't mean that they are true.

The mind is part of the soul, and for your soul to be healed, your mind also needs to be healed and renewed. The devil often comes against God's people on the battlefield of the mind, and he will try to influence your thoughts and use them to stop or slow down your healing journey.

The way to overcome and conquer the accuser is to believe God's promises more than we believe the lies the enemy puts in our minds. It is so important to remember that all of the thoughts that enter our minds are not necessarily true. Only God's Word is truth.

Revelation 12:11 tells us how to conquer the accuser—with the blood of the Lamb (Jesus) and the word of our testimony, which means knowing God's Word and letting it be your guide for life. It is also good to tell others what God has done for you. As a person whose soul is in the process of healing, part of your testimony is still being crafted. But part of it is already settled: You are a beloved, redeemed child of God, filled with potential! You are a miracle in the making, a masterpiece of God's handiwork. While you were still in sin, Jesus died for you (Rom. 5:8), so just imagine what He wants to do for you now that you have been forgiven and desire to grow in relationship with Him. No matter what you think or how things seem right now in your life, God's plans for your future will astound you!

God's great plans for your life will unfold day by day as you continue to live by His Word and let Him lead you. Remember this when the devil hurls accusations against you in your mind. Remind him of the blood of Jesus and the word of your testimony, which is that God is healing you and strengthening you more and more each day. Open the Word of God and read all the wonderful things God says about you instead of listening to the enemy's lies.

Declare this:

I overcome every accusation of the enemy by the blood of Jesus and the word of my testimony.

Let Your Tears Flow

As soon as I heard these words I sat down and wept and mourned for days, and I continued fasting and praying before the God of heaven.

Nehemiah 1:4

Nehemiah was not afraid of emotion or reluctant to show it. Notice that he "wept and mourned." Some people refuse to exhibit any kind of outward emotion, which is not healthy. Pent-up feelings are harmful and need to be released. If we do not release our emotions at appropriate times, as Nehemiah did when he heard the walls of Jerusalem had been destroyed, our emotions will eat away at us on the inside.

Stuffing or suppressing our feelings can also cause physical problems such as sleep troubles and digestive issues. Perhaps you have heard of people who went to the doctor because they felt so bad and were convinced something was wrong with them. Once they went through all kinds of medical tests, the doctor found nothing and simply said their symptoms were related to anxiety. Our emotions will always manifest in some way, so it's best for us to deal with them before they deal with us.

God created us with tear glands and the ability to cry, which must mean there will be times in life when we, like Nehemiah, need to weep. The Old Testament woman, Hannah, wept and even stopped eating because she was brokenhearted over not having a child (1 Sam. 1:7). When David and the men with him discovered the Amalekites had burned the city of Ziklag and taken everyone in it captive, they "raised their voices and wept until they had no more strength to weep" (1 Sam. 30:4). David also wept when his son became deathly ill (2 Sam. 12:21–22). Even Jesus wept over the death of His friend Lazarus (John 11:35).

Tears are certainly part of the process of healing in our soul. God speaks through the prophet Jeremiah: "Pour out your heart like water before the presence of the LORD" (Lam. 2:19). This assures us that God wants us to bring our pain to Him. We can tell Him everything about it, holding nothing back. He knows it all anyway, but getting it out in the open is very helpful to us.

Though it is important to express our deep feelings through tears at times, God did not create us to remain in a season of weeping indefinitely. There is "a time to weep, and a time to laugh" (Eccles. 3:4). God's Word promises us that "Weeping may endure for a night, but joy comes in the morning" (Ps. 30:5 NKJV). No matter what you are going through right now, ask God to help you deal with it in a healthy way. Cry when you need to, but always remember that the season of sadness will come to an end. As you walk with God, He will lead you into great joy.

Declare this:

I express my emotions in healthy ways, knowing that sadness will ultimately lead to joy.

Jesus Is the Best Kind of Helper

Although He was a Son, He learned [active, special] obe-dience through what He suffered and, [His completed experience] making Him perfectly [equipped], He became the Author and Source of eternal salvation to all those who give heed and obey Him.

Hebrews 5:8–9 AMPC

Have you ever tried to figure out how to make a gadget or an electronic device work properly? That kind of thing comes easily to people who know a lot about technology. But it can be very frustrating to people like me, who aren't technologically savvy and who just want the device to work! I have learned that if I accidentally hit the wrong button on my phone and start having trouble with it, all I need to do is look for a young person to help me. Though I am older and I have much more life experience than a sixth-grader who can fix my phone, that child has something I do not have: specific experience with today's technology. I may know a lot in some areas, but I can't fix my phone; I need help, and the best kind of helper is one with experience.

Jesus has all the experience required to help us along our

healing journey. Hebrews 5:8–9 speaks volumes to me not only about Him but also about my life and yours. Jesus needed certain experience in order to truly understand our pain and become our High Priest who can help us heal. My experience with Jesus' healing power makes me a good person to boldly tell others He will heal their wounded souls just as He has healed mine, and your experience will do the same for you.

Jesus suffered greatly and gained experience as a result. His experience equipped Him to fulfill what God wanted Him to do. Hebrews 4:15 says He is able "to understand and sympathize and have a shared feeling with our weaknesses" (AMPC) because He has already gone through the things we suffer. I hope you will think about this verse often and allow it to give you hope and confidence that what you are going through will enable you to help others.

I encourage you today, even at this moment, to offer your experience to God for His use if you have never done that. No matter how confusing, painful, or difficult it may be, He can use it to provide the experience you need to help someone else. I vividly remember praying one day, "God, I am a broken mess, but I'm Yours if You can use me." He did. He chose to use me in specific ways to help others, and I believe there is a specific way He wants to use you, too. Nothing we give to God is ever wasted, so give Him your pain today and see how He will use your experience.

Declare this:

I trust God to use my painful experiences to help and encourage others.

9

You Are Free to Be Yourself

Therefore, if anyone is in Christ, he is a new creation. The old has passed away; behold, the new has come.

2 Corinthians 5:17

When we have been deeply wounded in our soul, we can struggle with identity as a result, meaning that we go through life feeling we do not know who we truly are. This can cause us to feel confused, purposeless or directionless, empty and unsatisfied no matter how hard we try to find fulfillment. One reason our woundedness has such a negative effect on our identity is that it causes us to want to hide our true feelings and to hesitate to express who we really are. For example, if someone is afraid to be vulnerable, she may pretend to be tough, confident, and self-sufficient to keep others from viewing her as weak or needy. This type of pretending to be something we are not or presenting a certain image that does not accurately represent us can be a temptation to everyone who has been wounded. Our hunger for acceptance and approval may cause us to try to alter our personalities to try to be what we think people want us to be instead of feeling free to be our true selves.

The chameleon is a lizard-like animal that can change its color so it will blend in with everything around it. Chameleons do this to protect themselves. If their predators can't distinguish them from a log or a leaf, they can't hurt them. Although people cannot change colors, we have our own protective mechanisms, one of which is to develop false identities to guard ourselves against rejection or disapproval.

Those who fear rejection often become people pleasers, doing what they think others want them to do instead of becoming their true selves. That is sad, because we are never truly free until we are free to be ourselves.

The world urges us to conform to its image. It tells us what we should wear, how we should style our hair, what kind of car we should drive, how much education we need—and on and on. We sense intuitively that if we do not measure up to the world's standards, we will not be accepted.

God loves and accepts us unconditionally, and when we receive Jesus as our Savior, He makes us new. All the old pressures we have felt melt away. We no longer have to feel guilty about old mistakes. When God makes us new, we become like fresh lumps of spiritual clay. The world wants to fashion us in its image, but the Holy Spirit wants to mold us into something new, to shape us in such a way that we can fulfill God's amazing plans for our lives. In Christ, we are finally free to be our true selves, and that's the best person we can possibly be.

Declare this:

Because I am in Christ, everything old has passed away. God has made me new!

10

Believe and See

*"Therefore I tell you, whatever you ask in prayer, believe
that you have received it, and it will be yours."*

Mark 11:24

If we look at life without considering the promises of God, all we
have is what we see or feel. But with God's promises, what seems
impossible becomes possible. God's only requirement is that we
believe what He says more than we believe anything else. The
world says, "I won't believe until I see," but God says, "Believe and
then you will see."

What do you believe about yourself, your past, and your
future? Do you believe things will always be the way they have
always been? I hope not, because if things in your life have not
been good, that means you are stuck with that as your destiny.
Perhaps you didn't have a good beginning in life, but you can have
a great finish! I know that is true because God says in His Word
that He has a good plan for our future, one that should fill us with
hope (Jer. 29:11).

When people have been emotionally wounded, it adversely
affects how they think. Their thoughts are often negative, especially

about themselves and their life in general. They may live with what the Bible calls "evil forebodings," which is an expectation that something bad is going to happen. However, God's Word renews our minds. It teaches us how to think and to expect good things to happen. It gives us a new attitude that allows us to live with joy and hope rather than with sadness, depression, and discouragement. It takes time and patience to see the changes you desire, so don't expect things to change overnight.

God's Word has inherent power in it, and once we learn to think in agreement with God, we will see positive changes in our lives. But remember, believing must come before seeing. God told David he would be king, but twenty years passed before he wore the crown. David went through a lot of difficult testing of his faith while he waited, but at the right time, he did become king. Like David, at the right time you will be all God wants you to be and have all He wants you to have. Just continue believing God's promises and refuse to give up!

Ask God for things in prayer that are impossible and believe you will see them come to pass. While you wait for God to heal your wounded soul, stay busy helping and being kind to other people. The Bible tells us to "trust God and do good" (Ps. 37:3). Each morning, ask God to show you someone you can help that day, and as you do, your joy will increase and you will be sowing seeds for your own harvest.

Declare this:

I believe God's Word, no matter what my circumstances look like, and I expect to see all of God's good promises come to pass in my life.

11

The Painless Path

What comes easy won't last, and what lasts won't come easy.

Author Unknown

We frequently delay our own healing because we keep searching for a painless path. We want to get well, but we don't want it to hurt. That is understandable, but powerful things never come easily. What Jesus did for us didn't come easily.

I don't want to give you false hope, so I will openly tell you that if you have been abused, abandoned, rejected, or wounded through long-term illness or disappointments in life, your journey to healing won't be easy, but it will be worth it. The reason it is not easy is that you will have to open up areas of your life you may have kept hidden or stuffed somewhere deep inside you, refusing even to admit you are a wounded person.

Only the truth will set us free, but facing that truth may be one of the most difficult things we ever do. For example, all children want their parents to love them, and I found that even as an adult, I continued being hurt and disappointed by my parents because I kept trying to get something from them that they simply did not know how to give me.

One day I looked at myself in the mirror and said, "Joyce, your parents did not love you, and they never will. It wasn't your fault, so let it go and move on!" It hurt to face that, but it also set me free to stop frustrating and disappointing myself by trying to get something my parents couldn't or wouldn't give. They were both wounded themselves and did not even know what real love was.

You may have to face something about yourself that will be hard to do. I had to face that I was bitter, full of self-pity, selfish and self-centered, and controlling, just to mention a few. When God began to deal with me about these things, I assured Him that I had a very good reason for all of my bad behavior. After all, I had been abused! He let me know that although I did have a good reason, I had no right to continue behaving badly because He was willing to set me free. Letting go of feeling sorry for myself was hard for me because by then I was literally addicted to self-pity and it was my go-to emotion anytime I did not get my way. Thankfully, God continued dealing with me until I was free, and He wants to do the same for you.

God never allows more to come on us than we can bear, and you can be assured that if God is dealing with you about something, it is the right time to let go of something old and take hold of the new way of living He offers. You may not feel ready to face something painful, but the Holy Spirit, Who is your Helper, will be with you each step of the way, and He will strengthen and enable you to do it.

I encourage you to stop looking for an easy way and know in your heart that sometimes God has to lead us the long, hard way for our own good. You will learn things along the way that will be of great value to you in the future. Easy things never make you stronger, but difficult things do. Take God's hand and trust His guidance even if you don't understand it.

Declare this:

I am not afraid of difficulty because I know God enables me to do whatever I need to do in life.

Nothing Can Take God's Love from You

No, in all these things we are more than conquerors through him who loved us. For I am sure that neither death nor life, nor angels nor rulers, nor things present nor things to come, nor powers, nor height nor depth, nor anything else in all creation, will be able to separate us from the love of God in Christ Jesus our Lord.

Romans 8:37–39

What we all want more than anything else is to be loved and accepted unconditionally. If we have not received that by the time we are teens or young adults, we have wounded souls and are unable to function the way God intended. He created us for love and acceptance, not abuse and rejection.

The good news is that if we did not get what we needed and should have had from the people in our past, we can get it from God now, and it will heal us. My father, who abused me, told me he loved me, but his kind of love hurt, so I grew up needing, but being afraid, of love. I didn't trust people who said they loved me, and it was difficult for me even to learn to receive God's love because I felt as if I were damaged and not worth being loved.

When I finally let God into my wounds, one of the first things He began teaching me was that He loved me unconditionally. I finally accepted that He loved me, but I still felt it must come with conditions, so I worked hard at being perfect so I could deserve His love. You may have experienced or perhaps are experiencing the same thing. If the people who were supposed to love us didn't, then we are convinced there is something wrong with us that makes us unworthy of love. It actually took me a few years to become totally convinced of God's love for me to the point where nobody and nothing could take it away from me.

This never-ending, perfect love of God is available to you and me, and it is the most wonderful thing we could ever have. God's perfect love sets us free from fear (1 John 4:18). If you are anything like I was, you have many fears in your life, but you can be free from every one of them through learning to soak in God's love on a regular basis. You may feel fear, but if you know God's love, you won't have to obey fear. You can move forward even if you feel fear because you know that, no matter what, God will always be there for you. If you make a mistake, He will help you recover and keep moving forward.

God's love is the healing balm we need for our wounded souls. Study Scriptures about God's great love for you and learn to speak them aloud over your life. Before long, you will start believing the truth of God's Word, and it will heal you.

Declare this:
God loves me unconditionally, and I do not have to bow down to fear.

13

Loving God's Word

My son, be attentive to my words; incline your ear to my sayings. Let them not escape from your sight; keep them within your heart. For they are life to those who find them, and healing to all their flesh.

Proverbs 4:20–22

God's Words are life to us and they bring healing to every area of our life, including our inner life (soul). His Word is actually medicine for a wounded soul. Just as there are different types of medicines available for various disease and wounds of the physical body, God's Word is medicine that heals our minds, emotions, wills, attitudes, consciences, and behaviors. It has a positive effect on our joy, peace, and confidence. It can cure fear, insecurity, and negativity.

Just as we get a prescription from the doctor and patiently take our medicine as often as we are supposed to, and get it refilled when we need to, we should look at God's Word in the same way. For example, if we are fearful, there are countless Scriptures that will help us deal with fear, or if we are worried or anxious, we may turn to Scripture and find help. I am convinced that we do not have a problem for which God's Word doesn't have an answer.

Bible study may sound daunting to you, and if so, I recommend that you either join a Bible study group in which the Scripture is being explained, or find a pastor or Bible teacher who is very practical in their teaching and makes God's Word applicable to your everyday life. Don't simply say, "I try to read the Bible and I don't understand it." Be determined to find a way to understand it and begin by asking the Holy Spirit to help you learn something each time you open the Scripture to read it. After more than forty years I still do that each morning when I study. The Holy Spirit is our Teacher.

One of the things that helped me a lot was reading good Bible-based books in any area in which I needed help. I read books on rejection, shame, guilt, fear, worry, and emotional healing. Learn to study in the areas where you need help rather than just randomly opening the Bible and reading something in order to check your Bible reading off your list for the day.

Wounded, dysfunctional people have paid hundreds of thousands of dollars to go into treatment centers, or for professional counseling. Let me quickly add that both may be very good. But sometimes those same people won't pay twenty-five dollars for a Bible-based book from a Christian author or a small fee to attend a Christian conference that could be life-changing for them.

If you are serious about having a wounded soul healed, then you will need to develop a love for God's Word. See it for what it is! It is not merely words in black ink on white pages. It is life, healing, strength, courage, and anything else you need.

Declare this:

God's Word is my life and my strength, and I love it!

14

You Are Not Damaged Goods

In Him you have been made complete, and He is the head over all rule and authority.

Colossians 2:10 NASB

Women who have been abused in any way often feel they are damaged beyond repair. I grew up thinking no one would ever want me as a wife because of what my father had done to me, so I made the mistake of marrying the first boy who showed interest in me, at the age of eighteen, and he had even more problems than I did. After five more years of abuse from him, I got a divorce. Those five years were filled with pain I could have avoided had I not been so desperate to be loved and afraid I never would be.

No matter what has happened to you in the past, you are not damaged goods, because when we are in Christ, we become new creatures entirely and old things pass away (2 Cor. 5:17). As the Scripture says, we are "made complete" in Him. Whatever we did not get from people, we can get from God. He pays us back for all the mistreatment we have experienced in life, and then, in His goodness, He uses those painful things to help us help others. God makes us strong at our broken places!

How you see yourself is very important. It's more important than what anyone else thinks of you. God sees the end from the beginning, and believe me, no matter how bad your beginning was, you can have a great finish in your life. You cannot change the way things were, but you can go forward and never look back. People often think, *If only that hadn't happened to me, I would have a better life.* But you can still have a great life no matter what has happened to you, because God is an expert at fresh starts and new beginnings.

You may still be dealing with some of the effects of a painful past, but the time will come when there will be no evidence that they ever happened. I had my hip replaced a few years ago and it hurt for several weeks while it was healing. It gradually got better and better and now I can't even tell I ever went through that surgery. I have a new hip, and it is much stronger than the old one. God works in our souls the same way. When we open our wounds to Him and ask for healing, it hurts and the pain may get worse for a while, but gradually we get better and better and will eventually be stronger than ever.

If you believe you are damaged goods and that you will always have an inferior life, then that is what you will experience. God has promised us many wonderful things, but we access each of them by believing they are for us and receiving them by faith. Jesus died for you to have a wonderful, joyful, and peaceful life and I urge you not to settle for anything less.

Declare this:

I am complete in Christ, and I am a new person in Him. Old things have passed away and all things are made new.

15

Setting Boundaries

The fear of man lays a snare, but whoever trusts in the
Lord is safe.

Proverbs 29:25

It is wrong for anyone to try to control us, but it is equally wrong
for us to allow it. We must stand up for ourselves and be determined to please God rather than other people. My mother allowed
my father to control her out of fear, and everyone in the family paid
the price for her refusal to stand up for herself and us. Fear is a real
thing, but it has no power over us except what we give it. Author
and psychologist Henry Cloud says that we get what we tolerate.

The best thing is never to start a relationship by letting yourself be controlled and manipulated. But if you are already in that
situation, it is not too late to stand up for yourself. It will be more
difficult to do than it would have been had you had boundaries
from the beginning of the relationship, but it can still be done. Let
the person who is controlling you know that you realize you have
been allowing them to control you and that you will no longer let
it continue. They may react in an angry and even a violent manner, but in the end they will respect you for it.

It is God's will for us to follow the guidance of the Holy Spirit, and in order to do that, we will find that we must often say no to the demands of people. People who will only stay in relationship with you if they are allowed to control you don't really love you. They are simply using you to help them get what they want. You deserve better than that and are far too valuable to let anyone abuse or misuse you.

If you have a history of not speaking up or just "going along to get along," taking the first step toward freedom will be the most difficult. Satan is delighted to rob you of your God-ordained destiny, and he can easily do it through the fear of other people. The apostle Paul said that had he been trying to be popular with people, he would not have become an apostle of the Lord Jesus Christ (Gal. 1:10). Think seriously about that for a moment, and then take a look at your own life and make sure you are not missing God's will by being overly concerned about keeping people happy.

We should want to please and make people happy, but not if the price of doing so is disobeying God. The Word of God tells us to follow peace and I want to strongly recommend that you begin doing that. Anyone who truly cares about you will want you to follow God even if it means you can't give them what they want. God is always with you to help you do what you need to do.

Declare this:
I live to please God, not people!

16

You Are Loved

God's love has been poured into our hearts through the Holy Spirit who has been given to us.

Romans 5:5

One of the most powerful verses in the Bible is 1 John 4:8, which says, "Anyone who does not love does not know God, because *God is love*" (italics mine). In other words, God's very nature is love, and it is more powerful than anything else in the universe. All He has to offer us is love. Everything He does is rooted in love. And it is impossible for God to be anything but loving. Whenever you think about God, read about Him in His Word, or talk to Him, you can be certain that He loves you all the time.

The apostle Paul writes in Romans 5:5 that the love of God is poured out in our hearts through the Holy Spirit. When we choose Jesus as our Lord and Savior, the Holy Spirit comes to dwell in our hearts through faith as one of God's gifts to us. He does many things for us and works in our lives in various ways, one of which is to bring God's love to us and to remind us of it.

A person with a wounded soul may struggle to believe God loves her. She may feel she is not valuable enough to be loved by God or she may fear that God is like people who have said they loved her and then hurt her. But what God wants is for us to receive His love by faith, believing He is greater than our fears, our failures, our weaknesses, and the pain of our past.

When we are able to stand firm in the knowledge that God loves us, our hearts are filled with confidence, peace, joy, hope, concern for others, and positive attitudes toward our future.

I encourage you to ask the Holy Spirit to continue to reveal God's love to you in personal ways and to look up Scriptures about God's love. I also encourage you to memorize these Scriptures to help yourself become more firmly established in the fact that He loves you. Here are a few to get you started:

- "For God so loved the world, that he gave his only Son, that whoever believes in him should not perish but have eternal life" (John 3:16).
- "I have loved you with an everlasting love; I have drawn you with unfailing kindness" (Jer. 31:3 NIV).
- "But you, O Lord, are a God merciful and gracious, slow to anger and abounding in steadfast love and faithfulness" (Ps. 86:15).
- "But God shows his love for us in that while we were still sinners, Christ died for us" (Rom. 5:8).

As you meditate on these verses and others like them and ask the Holy Spirit to make them real and personal to you, you will grow in your confidence that God loves you.

Declare this:

Every day in every way, I know God loves me!

17

How to Rest Your Soul

Truly my soul finds rest in God; my salvation comes from him.

Psalm 62:1 NIV

Just as keeping our physical bodies healthy requires adequate rest, keeping our souls healthy requires allowing them to rest, too. When we are at complete rest in our mind, will, and emotions, only then will we be free from the tyranny of circumstances and people that upset us. Sometimes we face situations that keep our minds and emotions so tense that we can feel the weariness on the inside even if we are physically rested.

An easy way to rest the soul is to take a deep breath, get quiet, and focus on something else for a while. For example, you might say, "I am so upset about what's happening with my son, but right now I am going to focus on the fact that God loves him, God loves me, and God is bigger than this problem." If you are struggling with strife in your home, you might also choose to get outside and take a walk each day simply to remove yourself from a stressful atmosphere temporarily. While you're walking, don't let your mind dwell on the situation at home. Choose instead to think positive thoughts or to pray and thank God that He is working in your family and will bring peace as you follow Him. Sometimes when your soul is in turmoil, it's a good idea just to give it a break and watch a good, clean, funny movie. After all, "A merry heart does good, like medicine" (Prov. 17:22 KNJV).

A popular term these days is *self-care*. You can actually google "ideas for self-care," and you will be amazed at how many you can find. Many of these activities could also be called "soul care" because they are designed to help you find peace in the midst of life's busyness. But I would caution you against simply looking at a list and trying to work your way down it. Every idea isn't right for every person. For one woman, baking bread might be restful while another would find that stressful. One would truly enjoy sitting on a porch alone drinking tea or coffee, while others would be bored with that. Only you can determine what would bring rest to your soul. I encourage you to take some time today to think and pray about ways you can rest and care for your soul. The Holy Spirit will give you ideas and lead you to things that will be genuinely restful for you.

If you are not used to resting your soul, it may take time and practice to learn to do so. Don't get discouraged along the way. Remember that God will complete the good works He begins in you (Phil. 1:6). Just keep pressing on; don't give up. Eventually, little by little, your soul will find its rest.

Declare this:

I will remember to rest my soul, just as I rest my body, as the Holy Spirit leads me.

18

The Best Cure for the Soul

*Blessed (happy, favored by God) are those who hear the
Word of God and continually observe it.*

Luke 11:28 AMP

A woman can seek all kinds of help for emotional healing. She can
look to books or audiovisual materials, small groups at church,
individual or group therapy, or online resources. These things
may be effective, but one thing I can guarantee will always bring
health and strength to the soul is the Word of God. When we
study, believe, and obey the Word, amazing transformations take
place on the inside of us. No matter what we do, it will never fully
meet our needs if it is not based on God's Word. I know people
who have spent thousands of dollars on therapies and treatment
programs claiming to be able to change their lives, yet the healing
and deliverance they needed did not come until they made Jesus
their Lord and Savior and began to follow His path to freedom and
wholeness by obeying God's Word.

God's Word is filled with promises for those who act on what
He says to do, and these promises are for everyone who believes

and puts their trust in Him. Just think about these promises from Scripture:

- "The LORD is near to the brokenhearted and saves the crushed in spirit" (Ps. 34:18).
- "Fear not, for I am with you; be not dismayed, for I am your God; I will strengthen you, I will help you, I will uphold you with my righteous right hand" (Isa. 41:10).
- "'For the mountains may depart and the hills be removed, but my steadfast love shall not depart from you,' says the LORD who has compassion on you" (Isa. 54:10).
- "For I know the plans I have for you, declares the LORD, plans for welfare and not for evil, to give you a future and a hope" (Jer. 29:11).
- "Come to me, all who labor and are heavy laden, and I will give you rest. Take my yoke upon you, and learn from me, for I am gentle and lowly in heart, and you will find rest for your souls" (Matt. 11:28–29).
- "Do not be anxious about anything, but in everything by prayer and supplication with thanksgiving let your requests be made known to God. And the peace of God, which surpasses all understanding, will guard your hearts and your minds in Christ Jesus" (Phil. 4:6–7).

The desire and goal of everyone who hurts is to be healed. When we're in pain, there's nothing we want more than to get out of it! Knowing and believing God's promises is the best place to begin. You don't have to build the rest of your life on the pain of the past. You can start today to build it on the promises of God!

Declare this:

I believe that the Word of God is the one thing that will heal my soul!

19

The Pain Won't Last Forever

For this light momentary affliction is preparing for us an
eternal weight of glory beyond all comparison, as we look
not to the things that are seen but to the things that are
unseen.

2 Corinthians 4:17–18

Like you, I have faced difficult times in life, and I have learned to
tell myself, "This can't last forever. This, too, shall pass." When
you are going through hardship, deep disappointment, or some
struggle that seems impossible, it's easy to be tempted to think, *I*
cannot stand this for one more day.

The devil takes advantage of our hurts and wounds, and tempts
us to think several times a day that our trials are going to last forever, that we will hurt for the rest of our lives, or that the negative
effect of our problems will be permanent. We think, and sometimes fear, our pain will follow us everywhere we go for as long
as we live. The truth is, nothing on earth lasts forever. The only
thing we have that is eternal is our life in Christ. In the context of
eternity, the struggles that seem unending in this life are actually
quite brief. God always wants to heal us, restore us, and deliver us.

Chances are, you can look back over the course of your life and remember other times you have been hurt. God has been faithful to bring you through those times; you can be confident you will make it through this current challenge again through Christ, who gives you strength (Phil. 4:13).

Paul's point in 2 Corinthians 4:17–18 is that seasons of difficulty always pass. They do not last forever. Going through trials is tough, but God is always with us—helping us, encouraging us, and fighting our battles for us. He never wants us to stay in pain. He always wants to heal us.

When you are tempted to become discouraged because you feel your journey to healing in your soul is taking a long time, remember: "This, too, shall pass." Your afflictions may not seem "light and momentary" to you right now, but from the perspective of eternity, they are. No matter how difficult your situation may look, God loves you and has a good plan for your life. Your future is bright, and He is preparing you for something great.

Romans 8:28 says that we can "*know* that for those who love God *all* things work together for good, for those who are called according to his purpose" (italics mine). God can take even the hurts and wounds we endure and use them for good in our lives. They won't last forever, and He will use them to strengthen us and to bless and help others.

Declare this:

The situation I am currently facing will not last forever. God has a great plan for my life!

20

You Have All the Strength You Need

I can do all things through him who strengthens me.

Philippians 4:13

When our soul has been wounded, we do not always feel strong and capable. In fact, the opposite often happens. We feel weak. We aren't confident, and we can be easily intimidated. Instead of facing our challenges with courage, we would like to run and hide from them. None of this reflects the truth of who we are in Christ. The truth is that we have all of God's strength available to us all the time. We may feel weak in ourselves, but God's strength proves itself most effective when we lean and rely completely on Him. The key to strength is not working harder or trying to act strong when you are crumbling inside. It is in surrendering your heart to God and trusting Him.

Churches today are filled with people who know God. They are saved; they believe God is their Father; and they confess Jesus as Lord. But some of them do not know God as their source of strength. These believers are missing out on one of God's great gifts—His ability to strengthen, encourage, and empower us when we feel weak.

The apostle Paul must have felt weak at times because he wrote several verses about God's strength including today's Scripture, Philippians 4:13. We know that he struggled with some type of "thorn in the flesh" (2 Cor. 12:7) that bothered him. He wanted God to take it away, but instead God promised to give him the strength to endure it, saying, "My strength and power are made perfect (fulfilled and completed) and show themselves most effective in [your] weakness" (2 Cor. 12:9 AMPC).

It is understandable that you could feel weak when you have been deeply hurt in your soul. As God heals your soul, there will be times when you think you simply are not strong enough to confront or deal with the things that need to be dealt with. Naturally speaking, that is true. But you do not have to live according to natural reality. As a believer, you can live by spiritual truth. And the truth is that through the Holy Spirit, God will give you supernatural strength. He will make you strong to do the things you need to do in life and to fully walk the journey of healing that He is leading you on.

The way you see yourself is the way you will be. If you view yourself as weak, you will approach the situations you face in life from a position of weakness and insecurity. But God wants you to approach everything from your position of strength in Him. Begin to see yourself as strong because you are in Christ, and He is stronger than anyone or anything. You can draw strength from Him anytime you need it.

Declare this:

I can do all things through Christ because He gives me strength!

21

You're Not Alone

Whoever walks with the wise becomes wise.

Proverbs 13:20

Sometimes people who have been deeply wounded use the pain or abuse they went through to excuse current behavior that is not right. Other times, people who have suffered deep hurts want to hide their pain because they are ashamed of it. This is especially true for those who have endured sexual abuse. I know about this firsthand, because my father sexually abused me for years when I was a child.

After Dave and I had been married about five years, we attended a seminar at our church. The speaker shared her testimony about being sexually abused by her father. I did not know ahead of time that she would be speaking on that subject, and hearing her story brought to the surface pain that I had hidden in my heart for a long time.

Wanting to help me heal from my past, Dave bought the woman's book about her testimony for me. Reading her story made me angry because it reminded me of what I had been through. Obviously, I was still in pain, though I had tried to bury it for years.

Whatever your situation is, I want you to know that someone else has been through it, too. Just as the seminar speaker was ahead of me on the journey to healing from sexual abuse, someone has gone before you on your journey, too. That woman had learned keys to healing that I needed, and she was willing to share them in her book.

Let me encourage you today to find books, blogs, audio or video messages, or Internet posts from people who have experienced the same struggles you have faced. Let the healing God has done in their lives encourage you, and allow the fact that they have moved beyond their pain to inspire you to keep moving beyond yours. One of the gifts of being a believer in Jesus Christ is that we are part of God's family. And God uses people in His family to help and strengthen others.

You certainly don't want to run around and tell your story to anyone who will listen, especially if it is a sensitive matter. But if you ask God to send wise, trustworthy people into your life to help you, He will do it. One of the best ways to stay wounded is to remain isolated in your pain, and one of the best ways to be healed is to be willing to talk with others to learn how God has healed them. He may not heal you the same way He has healed them, but your healing and victory will be just as complete.

Declare this:

I am not alone on my journey to healing in my soul. Others have walked it and come through victorious, and so will I!

22

Your Journey Is Unique

I praise you, for I am fearfully and wonderfully made.
Wonderful are your works; my soul knows it very well.

Psalm 139:14

Do you ever stop and think about how unique and special you are? When our soul is wounded, we don't always feel special. Sometimes we feel very bad about ourselves and we feel unloved or unlovable. But everyone God creates is "fearfully and wonderfully made," and He loves each of us more than we can comprehend.

Just like the stars in the sky, every one of us is different. We are all born with different personalities, different likes and dislikes, different gifts and abilities, different physical features—even different fingerprints! Each of us has a special part to play in God's overall plan.

A lot of people have suffered wounds in their soul. The pain has some similarities, such as feelings of disappointment, rejection, or hopelessness, but people handle it differently. Some try to bury their pain, pretending that the situations that caused it never happened. Some express it in unhealthy ways, such as addictions or excessive behaviors. And some people have learned to deal with it in healthy ways.

People choose to handle their pain differently, and God chooses to heal our pain differently. One woman's journey to healing will not be like her mother's, her sister's, or her friend's. When God begins to heal us, we cannot assume He will do it the same way He healed someone else, but we can always be sure He will do it in the way that is best for us. All we need to do is discover how He is leading us and follow Him down that path.

God chooses to heal some people in the context of a Bible study or small group from church. He chooses to heal others in more private settings, maybe by spending time with a pastor or Christian counselor. Some people find healing in nature. Others find it in creating art or sculpture. No matter what your journey to healing looks like, I can assure you of two things.

First, your journey will be designed by God just for you. In His deep knowledge and love for you, He will lead you in a way that is right for you.

Second, your journey will be based on His Word. He may lead you to study a specific book of the Bible, such as Ephesians or John. He may lead you to study certain portions of Scripture, such as Psalms or Proverbs. Or He may impress on your heart that you should study Bible verses on specific topics that will help you heal, topics such as receiving God's love, trusting God, forgiving others, finding peace, finding joy, or many other subjects. I encourage you to pray and ask God to reveal the unique journey He has for you. Follow Him wholeheartedly, and great things will happen!

Declare this:
I will follow God on the unique healing journey He has planned just for me.

23

The Power of Gratitude

Give thanks in all circumstances; for this is the will of God in Christ Jesus for you.

1 Thessalonians 5:18

When you are hurting, it might seem like being thankful is a difficult thing to do, but being thankful is very powerful. No matter what has been done to us that is unjust, God will bring justice and has promised to even give us double for our former trouble (Isa. 61:7). We all have things to be thankful for, no matter how many difficulties we might be facing. Focusing on what is good in your life will really help because what we focus on becomes larger than what we don't focus on.

Focusing on, thinking about, and talking about your pain and the injustices done to you only make them seem larger and more impossible to deal with. I can promise you from God's Word and my experience, as well as the experience of many others, that God won't let you down. He will bring justice; He will pay you back for what you have lost or missed out on in life. No one can tell you exactly when that will happen, but while you wait, be thankful and know that God's timing in your life will be perfect.

Not only is being thankful a good and powerful thing to do, it is God's will that we do so. You may not feel like being thankful, but do it on purpose and do it often. It will make you feel better and your joy will increase because you are focusing on something positive.

You can even thank God for things that have not happened yet, believing that He is faithful and that the reality of His promises will soon be seen in your life. You can thank God that He is working in your life, and that His justice is on its way to you. You can thank God that your past doesn't have to define you, because you know that He has a good future planned for you.

Usually we want to see something before we will believe it is true, but God requires that we believe and trust in His Word even before we see the answer to our prayer. Jesus said that if we believe, we will see the glory of God (John 11:40). God's Word says that we should be anxious for nothing, but in all things pray with thanksgiving (Phil. 4:6). Be sure to notice that He said, "Pray with thanksgiving." Anyone can ask God for something they want, but spiritual maturity is required for someone to be thankful before they get what they want.

I can assure you that God is working in your life right now. You may not feel anything or see anything changing, but in time you will. You have many victories that are on their way to you, so don't give up. God may deliver us little by little but each little victory is one step closer to total restoration.

Declare this:

I am grateful for what God has done, is doing, and will do in my life.

24

Only God

Let me ask you only this: Did you receive the Spirit by works of the law or by hearing with faith? Are you so foolish? Having begun by the Spirit, are you now being perfected by the flesh?

Galatians 3:2–3

There are many situations that we want to change, but they are completely beyond our control. There are times we want to change other people, but we are powerless over them. There are also times we want to change ourselves, especially when we are hurting. We simply want the pain in our hearts to go away or we want the struggle we are dealing with to end. We want to think differently, to feel differently, and sometimes to live differently! But we can't change ourselves either. We can't heal ourselves; we can't strengthen ourselves. All of that is God's job, and He will do it as we surrender to Him and trust Him. He will work with us patiently and lovingly, to lead us to the very best He has for us.

The apostle Paul understood this well. He knew the power of God's grace in such an intense, personal way because of his radical encounter with Jesus (Acts 9:1–22). God changed him from a vicious persecutor of Christians to one of the true heroes of our faith. He transformed Paul's heart completely! Because of his experience, he could say with authority that only God can change a person.

In Paul's letter to the Galatians, he makes several important points. One of them is what he says in Galatians 3:2, when he asks the Galatians whether they received the Spirit by works or by faith. Of course, he knew the Galatians received the Holy Spirit by faith. He asked the question because he wanted them to think about it. Everything God does for us, we receive by faith. We receive Christ totally by faith; we receive the Holy Spirit by faith; we receive the love of God by faith, and we need to live our lives totally by faith.

When we realize we need to change in some area—whether that change means we need to be healed and strengthened, or whether we should think or act differently—our natural response is to try to make that change happen. Our human nature thinks, "I will change!" Often we become very disappointed with ourselves, and we even feel condemned when we do not succeed at transforming ourselves. We would be much wiser to devote the energy we use trying to change ourselves to praying and trusting God to do what He needs to do.

You may be thinking right now of something you wish you could change about yourself. You are certainly responsible to do what God shows you to do and to be obedient as He leads you to change, but both the process of change and the end result are up to Him. He is working in you, and He will bring about the changes needed in your life as you continue to surrender to Him and follow Him.

Declare this:

Only God has the power to change me, and He will do it as I follow Him.

25

You Are God's Ambassador

*Therefore, we are ambassadors for Christ, God making
his appeal through us. We implore you on behalf of Christ,
be reconciled to God.*

2 Corinthians 5:20

Can you imagine how you would feel right now if you knew that
the pain in your soul could not only be healed completely, but
could also help other people? It can! In fact, that's part of God's
plan for your healing. When He heals our soul, He does a lot more
than simply relieve us of the ache in our hearts and the torment in
our minds; He transforms us in such a way that we become strong
in the place we were once weak and gives us the ability to help
others because of the way He has helped us.

My father abused me when I was young, and for a long time
that abuse had a negative impact on me. Since God healed me,
though, I have been able to help others because I went through
that experience. The same thing happens when a mother who has
had a wayward child then sees that child return to the Lord and
to the family. It happens when people lose a good job only to end
up with a better one. It takes place in all kinds of situations, and

every time God heals or restores, the person who has received that blessing from Him has a chance to encourage others by telling them about it. God takes bad things that have happened to us and works them out for our good (Rom. 8:28).

When you have personally suffered in some area in the past, you have a lot of credibility with people who may be struggling with it right now. They will listen to you and many times they will take your advice if they know you have already walked the journey they are currently on. When God heals your soul, it's not just for you. It's also so you can help and support others. You become an ambassador of God's grace, a person who can share what He has done for you. Nothing helps us understand someone in pain more than having had the same pain ourselves.

I hope you will begin today to think beyond your pain and believe God can use you—not in spite of it, but *because* of it. God turns everything that happens to us into something that eventually works for good (Rom. 8:28). What may seem bad to you today can become part of the good plan He has for your life. The pain you have been through and the healing God is doing in your life will make you a powerful ambassador for Him.

Next time you encounter people who are struggling with a situation God has brought you through or is currently bringing you through, ask Him how you can encourage that person and share with them the hope He has given you. You might tell them about specific Scriptures that have ministered to you or recommend Christian books or teachings to them. You could also speak a blessing or word of encouragement or do an act of kindness for them as the Holy Spirit leads you.

When God heals a heart, it's an awesome work, one that definitely blesses the person who has been healed and one that can help others, too.

Declare this:

I will be a powerful ambassador for God because of the healing He is doing in my heart.

26

You Can Enjoy Your Life

And God saw everything that he had made, and behold, it was very good. And there was evening and there was morning, the sixth day.

Genesis 1:31

When God had completed His six days of creation, He took time to look over everything, and according to the Amplified Bible, He saw that "it was very good and He validated it completely" (Gen. 1:31). By this time in the creation story, God had already created man and woman (Gen. 1:27). So when He pronounced that everything was "very good," it included Adam and Eve, who represent all of humanity. Everyone God made is good, including you and me.

Many people feel worthless, insecure, and unacceptable, which does not agree with God's opinion of us. He validates us completely. God knows everything about each of us, and He loves us unconditionally. God approves of us; He may not approve of everything we do, but He does approve of who we are as His beloved children. He does not want us to go through life discouraged, disappointed, wounded, or feeling bad about ourselves. He wants us to think about ourselves like He thinks of us.

Throughout His Word, God lets us know what He thinks about us. It says we are "fearfully and wonderfully made" (Ps. 139:14). It says He rejoices over us with gladness and quiets us with His love (Zeph. 3:17). It promises that He has good plans for us (Jer. 29:11) and that He will complete the good work He has begun in us (Phil. 1:6). It calls us the apple of His eye (Ps. 17:8). And it says that He loves us with an everlasting love (Jer. 31:3). Hopefully you can see that God approves of and enjoys you.

I encourage you to approve of and enjoy yourself as well. This may take some time for you, especially if you have been deeply wounded or if you have experienced things that have made you feel unlovable, unacceptable, or inferior to others. Never base what is true on your feelings, because they don't always agree with God's Word.

I had to reach a point in my life where I had to decide to agree with what God's Word says about me, even though I could have viewed myself as "damaged goods" as a result of sexual abuse by my father. Choosing to enjoy and accept myself is one of the best decisions I have ever made. God does not create anything worthless. He is good, and everything He does is good. We cannot believe that God created us and also believe we are worthless. Begin to accept and enjoy yourself where you are, and God will help you get to where you need to be.

Declare this:

I choose to agree with God, and I believe that I am very good!

27

It's Time to Let Go

Remember not the former things, nor consider the things of old. Behold, I am doing a new thing; now it springs forth, do you not perceive it? I will make a way in the wilderness and rivers in the desert.

Isaiah 43:18–19

When you are on the journey of having your soul healed, there comes a time when you have to make some critical decisions in order to move forward in a healthy way. In fact, making those decisions is a guaranteed way to make progress. One of them is to live according to God's Word in every situation. One is to forgive those who have hurt you. And one is to let go of the past and dare to believe God has a great future in store for you.

People try to hold on to the past in different ways, but we must remember that the past is past and no amount of holding on to it will change it. We should enjoy each day that we have right now, and we cannot do that if we are living in the past. Enjoy today while looking forward to a great future. Expect something good to happen to you!

There are all kinds of physical, emotional, and mental reasons why people will not let go of the past. Sometimes they feel the past was wonderful and they don't see how anything else could ever be so good, so they live in the past instead of enjoying the present and feeling hopeful about the future. Sometimes they can no longer do the things they once did, and instead of realizing their value in the present, they rest on their accomplishments from previous years.

As an example, let's think about a great football quarterback who won championships and became known as one of the greatest of all time. In the height of his career, he sustained an injury so serious he could never play football again. For years afterward, he talked about "the good ol' days" and how much he loved playing football, scoring touchdowns, and beating other teams. His sons and grandsons begged him to tell them how to throw, and the local high school team invited him to coach their young quarterback or even to give a motivational speech. He never did any of that because he was stuck in the past, unwilling to accept what had happened to him, let it go, and move forward.

Not all life-changing injuries affect the physical body. Debilitating things can also impact our minds and break our hearts. When those things happen, just like the quarterback, we can choose to fix our eyes on what life was like for us before those events and dwell on them for years, or we can decide to take Isaiah's advice and not remember the past. We can look ahead in faith that God is doing a new thing and that the days before us can be better than the ones behind us.

Declare this:

I choose today to let go of the past and embrace the bright future God has for me.

28

Step-by-Step Obedience

Now the LORD said to Abram, "Go from your country and your kindred and your father's house to the land that I will show you."

Genesis 12:1

The Old Testament man we call "Abraham" was a man of great faith. Having faith comes more easily to some people than to others simply because of the way they are wired, but I don't think anyone is born with the tremendous faith that Abraham had. It has to be developed over time, as we see God prove Himself faithful in one situation after another. God gives all of us a measure of faith, but our faith grows, like Abraham's, over time as we learn to trust God to lead us one step at a time. We do have to face difficult and challenging situations, but they become the tools that God uses to stretch our faith to new levels.

Abraham's first step of faith was to leave his home and his family, not knowing where to go next. All God said was that He would show him the right place, and Abraham trusted that and obeyed. He had to do the first thing God told him before God would tell him anything else.

By the time Abraham's faith was truly tested, he had developed such complete trust in God that he was willing to sacrifice his own son—the son God had promised him with his wife, Sarah, and the son he had believed God for and had waited for, for a very long time. When God asked him to sacrifice his son, he obeyed. But before he could do it, God spoke to him and told him not to. He even provided a ram in a nearby thicket so that Abraham would have an animal to sacrifice instead (Gen. 22:1–14). We have to wonder if Abraham would have had the faith to sacrifice his son had he not seen God prove Himself faithful on each step of his journey to that point.

Abraham's story is very dramatic when it gets to the part about sacrificing his son. I haven't heard of another story like that in history, but it is a great example for us as we walk the journey of healing in our soul. We would like for God to heal us instantly, but that's not the way it works. God strengthens and restores us little by little, one step at a time, and each time He does, our trust in Him grows.

As God heals our soul, there are times He is gracious enough to take us forward in a seemingly miraculous way, but there comes a time for everyone when He requires us to walk through a difficulty because that is the only way we will gain strength. There are many people who simply refuse to take the first step until they see every step along the way. But the best way to follow God as He heals your soul is to take each step He leads you to take when He leads you to take it, without questioning or hesitating. Once you take one step and see the faithfulness of God, you will have more faith for the second step than you had for the first. As the cycle continues, you will find yourself making great progress on your journey of healing.

Declare this:

I am committed to take each step God calls me to take, trusting Him to lead me where He knows I need to go.

29

Rooted and Grounded

May He grant you out of the riches of His glory, to be strengthened and spiritually energized with power through His Spirit in your inner self, [indwelling your innermost being and personality], so that Christ may dwell in your hearts through your faith. And may you, having been [deeply] rooted and [securely] grounded in love, be fully capable of comprehending with all the saints (God's people) the width and length and height and depth of His love [fully experiencing that amazing, endless love].

Ephesians 3:16–18 AMP

One of the great truths of our faith as Christians is that Jesus Himself lives in our hearts and we can be secure in His love. Believing that Jesus lives in our hearts is not necessarily something we can explain or understand with our minds, but it is something we receive by faith. No matter what happens in our lives, Jesus is with us because He lives in us. When you feel happy, He is there. When you feel lonely, afraid, weary, or hopeless, He is there. You can talk to Him and hear from Him at any time, in any place, under any circumstance.

Just think about a large, old, sturdy tree with its vast root system underground. Most of the time, we would look at such a tree and not even think about its roots. But if a big storm comes and that tree stands firm when other things have been uprooted and tossed about, we realize that its strength is in its roots. The deeper the roots are, the more difficult it will be for the forces of nature to destroy the tree. This helps us understand why Paul would pray for us to be deeply rooted in God's love. He knows the storms of life will come, but they will not damage or destroy us if our roots are deep in God's love.

Paul also prays that we will be securely grounded in God's love. The word *grounded* has several definitions, one of which refers to electrical systems. I learned on the Internet that a grounded electrical system makes it easier for the proper amount of power to be distributed to all the right places. God certainly wants His power to flow through us. Paul encourages us in Ephesians 3:16 to be "spiritually energized with power through His Spirit," and when we are grounded in His love, His power flows properly and in ways that help and encourage us and the people around us.

I encourage you to take time today to meditate on Ephesians 3:16–18. When Christ lives in your heart through faith, nothing—no storm of life, no pain from the past, no wound in your soul today—can uproot you from His love for you. Thank God for that, and pray that He will give you more and more understanding of what it means to have Christ living in your heart, rooting you and grounding you in His love.

Declare this:

Christ lives in me, and I am rooted deeply and grounded securely in His love.

30

A Shame-Free Life

I sought the LORD, and he answered me and delivered me from all my fears. Those who look to him are radiant, and their faces shall never be ashamed.

Psalm 34:4–5

When a woman has been wounded in her soul, sometimes hurt and pain are not the only things that result. Sometimes, depending on the type of wound, she can end up in shame—ashamed of what has happened to her and even ashamed of who she is. She may think what happened to her is her fault, or took place because of something flawed in her.

Shame makes a person feel dirty, unattractive, awkward, devalued, and unlovable. Often shame causes us to feel we are unworthy of having hopes and dreams, and it causes us to lose confidence doing things we would otherwise feel strong and comfortable about doing. It can poison our thoughts, feelings, and decisions to the point that we become withdrawn and hopeless. If I had to summarize briefly what shame does, I would say that it makes us feel like something is wrong with us, though we may not be able to pinpoint exactly what it is.

The things that wound our souls can leave a complicated set of consequences in our lives, and shame is often added to them. Especially in situations of sexual abuse, shame is only one of many results of being violated. I know this from personal experience, and I also know that it is possible to break free from shame completely. It is so important that we learn to do this, because if we don't, we will not be able to fully enjoy the life Jesus died to give us.

Our own thoughts and feelings can easily keep us trapped in shame, but God's Word sets us free. Jesus promises in John 8:32 that we will know the truth and the truth will make us free. This means we can be free from everything that holds us captive, including shame.

I want to remind you of two more of God's promises today as a way of encouraging you to be confident that you do not have to live in shame any longer. God says through Isaiah, "Fear not, for you will not be ashamed; be not confounded, for you will not be disgraced; for you will forget the shame of your youth" (Isa. 54:4). In case you're wondering, the word *confounded* means ashamed, defeated, confused, or overthrown. It also means damned, or doomed to punishment. That's not a good way to feel, but when we are ashamed of who we are, we can easily feel doomed and defeated. God does not want us to feel that way! And in the short Book of Zephaniah, He says, "Behold, at that time I will deal with all your oppressors. And I will save the lame and gather the outcast, and I will change their shame into praise and renown" (3:19).

God wants you to live a shame-free life, full of faith, confidence, peace, and joy. Stay in His Word and fill your mind with God's promises, and He will help you leave your shame behind you.

Declare this:

God's Word is truth. Truth sets me free, and I am totally free from shame.

31

God Works Miracles

Ah, Sovereign LORD, you have made the heavens and the earth by your great power and outstretched arm. Nothing is too hard for you.... Great and mighty God, whose name is the LORD Almighty, great are your purposes and mighty are your deeds.

Jeremiah 32:17–19 NIV

It is always good to stir up our faith and remember that God is a God of miracles. As the prophet Jeremiah said, *nothing* is too difficult for Him! Because we believe His Word, we can be confident that "with God all things are possible" (Matt. 19:26). You may feel that your life is a mess right now and that nothing will ever change. For a believer, that's just not true. God can take your biggest mess and turn it into your biggest miracle.

In our natural minds, there are certain things we think of as too difficult for us. You may be thinking about a situation right now that seems too hard for you. Maybe it's getting out of debt. Maybe it's losing weight and becoming physically healthy. Maybe it's doing your part to see a breakthrough in your marriage or family. Whatever your circumstances are, if there is something that seems too difficult for you, I have good news today: *It's not too hard for God.*

Let me remind you that in the Old Testament, God reached down from heaven and parted the Red Sea so His people could escape their enemies and walk through it on dry land (Exod. 14:21–22). If you or I were to visit the ocean, we would not be able to hold back even a handful of water, but God held back *all* of it. This miraculous deliverance positioned His people to finally enter into the great promises He had for them!

Think also about how hard you may have tried to change yourself or to change other people at times. That is very hard to do! But God can take hard, wounded, sinful, bitter hearts, and make them soft, whole, strong, holy, loving, and forgiving. If He can do that, then I believe He can do anything. The salvation and transformation He does in us is truly miraculous.

In the New Testament, Jesus did all kinds of miracles. Nothing was too difficult for Him—not turning five loaves and two fish into a meal that fed five thousand people (Mark 6:41–44), not healing a woman who had been bleeding for twelve years (Luke 8:43–48), not raising someone from the dead (Luke 8:49–55), not even walking on water (Matt. 14:22–25). All of these things would definitely be too hard for us, but not for Him.

I encourage you to spend some time thinking about the things you think are too hard for you. Take each one and surrender it to God. Release it and tell Him that you trust Him with it completely and that you believe nothing is too difficult for Him.

Declare this:

Nothing is too hard for God. He can work miracles in my life!

32

Moving Forward

Thus says the L<small>ORD</small>, your Redeemer, the Holy One of Israel: "I am the L<small>ORD</small> your God, who teaches you to profit, who leads you in the way you should go."

Isaiah 48:17

An important aspect of the healing of the soul is finding the courage to move beyond our pain. We may not be able to avoid all the hurts we face in life, but we can decide that we will not let them keep us from moving ahead. Sometimes when we are very wounded, we are tempted for various reasons to stay stuck in the pain, even though we can see that life is moving forward all around us. We can join in and go with what is happening, or we can stay behind, stuck in bitterness, resentment, hard-heartedness, and pain.

There are many reasons why people stay stuck in their pain. Maybe the "wounded person" has become their identity and they even use it to get attention. Maybe they fear they will fail if they try to do something new. Maybe they do not feel strong enough to move forward. Or maybe their self-image has been damaged to the point that they have no confidence in themselves and no confidence that God will take care of them if they move into something new.

We can always choose to stay in our pain, but that will not lead to the good things God has for us. Jesus died to give us a life of abundance, but we can choose whether to embrace it or not. If we want what He has, we have to make the choice to move beyond our pain and risk following Him.

I once saw a movie about a very talented woman who suffered such deep wounds in her soul that she completely withdrew from life and from other people. After a stay in a mental health facility, she literally parked her van in someone's driveway and lived in it for the rest of her life. The movie was a powerful picture of what can happen to people who either don't know how to or will not deal with their pain, leave the past behind, and move ahead.

God will never park us in our pain and leave us there, and I hope we never allow ourselves to park in it either. He is always calling us forward. He never leaves us alone to figure out on our own how to move ahead. He makes the path clear to us and leads us, as Isaiah 48:17 says, in the way that we should go. He promises to bring hope, healing, strength, and restoration to our lives if we will believe His Word and trust Him to lead us. Plenty of people in the Bible chose to leave their pasts behind and follow God into something new. And you can too!

Declare this:

I will not park in my place of pain. I trust God to lead me into healing and wholeness, and I choose to follow Him.

33

You Are Loved and Accepted

*Blessed be the God and Father of our Lord Jesus Christ,
who has blessed us in Christ with every spiritual blessing
in the heavenly places, even as he chose us in him before
the foundation of the world, that we should be holy and
blameless before him.*

Ephesians 1:3–4

One of the toughest battles many women fight inside themselves is the battle against rejection. They struggle, sometimes quite intensely, to believe they are loved and accepted. This can happen because of the way we see ourselves or the way we believe other people see us.

All kinds of people and situations can cause us to feel rejected or unworthy and have low self-esteem, but God wants us to know that He loves and accepts us unconditionally. The apostle Paul actually says that when we are in Christ, we are "holy and blameless" before God. That's the way He sees us, so that's the way we should see ourselves.

Sometimes, the people around us contribute to our low self-image by the way they treat us or speak to us. But God never, ever views us as anything but loved and accepted. Because we are in Christ, He sees us as flawless. This doesn't mean we have never sinned or done anything wrong; it simply means that when we are in Christ and we repent of our sins, God forgives us completely and we are clean before Him.

The Old Testament woman Leah was not an attractive person, and her father, Laban, thought no one would ever want to marry her. So when Jacob arranged with Laban to work for him for seven years in exchange for marrying the woman he was in love with— Leah's beautiful sister Rachel—Laban agreed. But on the wedding night, Laban sent Leah—instead of Rachel—to Jacob. There was no electricity in those days, so it was dark and Jacob didn't know the difference. He was very upset the next morning when he discovered Laban had tricked him (Gen. 29:16–25).

Just imagine how rejected Leah must have felt, knowing that her own father thought the only way she would ever marry would be for him to deceive someone. In addition, she knew Jacob was in love with her sister, not with her. In the end, God blessed Leah with children much more than He blessed Rachel, but the damage to Leah's self-esteem must have been severe.

Like Leah, you may feel rejected at times, but that is a lie from the enemy. The truth is that you are loved more than you can comprehend. Even when you think badly about yourself, God always thinks the best about you. The apostle Paul asked, "If God is for us, who can be against us?" (Rom. 8:31). Choose to believe today that God is for you, because He is! Choose to believe He accepts you fully, because He does! Choose to believe He loves you unconditionally and has a great plan for your life, because that's the truth!

Declare this:

I am completely accepted, approved of, and loved by God, and He is for me.

34

You Can Talk to God

I acknowledged my sin to You, and I did not hide my wickedness; I said, "I will confess [all] my transgressions to the LORD"; and You forgave the guilt of my sin.

Psalm 32:5 AMP

Our soul can be wounded for many reasons. Sometimes, we are wounded because of things other people have done to us. Sometimes, the wounds come from our own bad choices. Even when we regret past sin or mistakes, the pain they caused will linger if we let it.

Some people who are very strong Christians and walk closely with God today will tell you that they have not always had an intimate relationship with Him. Some of them, like me, have abuse, betrayal, addictions, and other hurtful things in their background. They are healed today because they refused to allow their past to determine their future. I want you to know that no matter what is in your past or how painful it has been, healing is available for you and your future can be better than you ever imagined.

One of the most important steps you can take toward the healing of your soul is to talk to God about what hurts you and confess to Him any sin you have committed. If there is shame or guilt associated with what happened to you (as in the case of victims of abuse or in the case of someone who made a very bad decision that affected others), you may wonder if God really wants to hear about it. I can assure you that He does. First of all, He knows everything about the situation anyway. And second, He understands that acknowledging our wrongdoing helps cleanse it from our soul. There is no one better than God to talk to about the things that have hurt you. You can talk to God about anything, and He will not judge you or be angry or frustrated with you. He loves you more than anyone on earth ever could, and He is the only one with the power to heal your broken heart.

Many people in the Bible sinned and failed. Some of those we think of as being closest to God made bad choices. Abraham got tired of waiting for God to give him a son through Sarah, so he turned to her handmaid instead (Gen. 16:1–4). David lusted after Bathsheba and got her pregnant, then had her husband killed (2 Sam. 11:2–24). But both Abraham and David recovered and went on to do great things for God. James refers to Abraham as "a friend of God" (James 2:23), and the Bible calls David a man after God's own heart (Acts 13:22).

One of the keys of David's restoration and the great future he enjoyed after his moral failure was his willingness to repent and receive God's forgiveness. He wrote that God desires truth in our innermost being (Ps. 51:6 AMP). I encourage you today to talk to God about the things that have hurt you or the ways you have failed in the past, and He will comfort you. You can be restored completely, and I encourage you to believe that with all your heart.

Declare this:

I will talk to God about everything, holding nothing back.

35

Bear One Another's Burdens

Bear one another's burdens, and so fulfill the law of Christ.
Galatians 6:2

If you have ever had a heavy burden to carry in life, you know what a blessing it is to feel that someone cares about you and is willing to help you bear it.

When your soul is wounded, the enemy takes advantage of it in all kinds of ways, one of which is to try to get you overly self-focused. He wants you to think about all the things that are wrong with you and everything that is bad in your life. He will try to fill your mind with only three words: *me, myself,* and *I.*

One of the ways God heals the soul is by helping us get our minds off ourselves and onto what we can do for other people. In fact, thinking of others, helping and supporting them, are keys to healing and wholeness. We might say that helping others is the best way to help ourselves.

When we read the words *bear one another's burdens,* it can seem like a difficult and weighty thing to do. But if we ask God to lead us, He will help us realize there are many ways to help people who are carrying heavy loads in life and that helping bear their burdens does not have to become burdensome to us. For example:

- Do you know a single mother who struggles financially? Maybe you could give her a gift card to a restaurant, so she could take her children out to eat. Or maybe she would like a gift card for a massage or a manicure while you watch her children or pay a trustworthy babysitter.
- Do you know someone who is caring for an elderly parent, day in and day out? Maybe you could give that person a break by offering to stay with the parent for several hours a week or by running errands. Perhaps the caregiver would also enjoy a free afternoon to just sit and read or have some quiet time to spend with God.
- Do you have a friend struggling with illness or recovering from a major operation? He or she might need transportation to doctors' visits, treatments, or therapy. Some people who are unable to participate in daily life due to health problems also appreciate visits from people who can let them know what is going on at church, at the office, or in the community. Asking people what they need and what they would like to talk about can be a great blessing.

Other simple ways to bear someone's burden include taking time for a cup of coffee and offering a listening ear, praying for people, sharing encouraging truths from God's Word, and other acts of kindness and thoughtfulness. Even one sentence such as, "I'm believing for God's best for you!" can be very encouraging.

As you trust God to heal your soul, I hope you will also do whatever you can do to help others bear their burdens, and remember, "Every time you help someone else, you help yourself."

Declare this:

I am available to help people with their difficulties in life, even if it means a sacrifice for me.

36

Don't Take the Blame

*Therefore there is now no condemnation [no guilty ver-
dict, no punishment] for those who are in Christ Jesus
[who believe in Him as personal Lord and Savior].*

Romans 8:1 AMP

Sometimes we feel pain in our soul because we have hurt other
people inadvertently. Often we hurt those people because we were
hurting, too, and we did not mean to wound them. This is especially true for women who may have been abused or otherwise
hurt while growing up, and then they in turn hurt their children.
They never wanted to cause problems; they simply did not know
any better. The same could be said for people who hurt friends,
spouses, or other family members unintentionally.

As we mature and come to realize that something we said or
did caused pain or struggle in another person's life, we may feel
very badly about it. When that happens, the thing to do is talk
to the person, admit what we have done to cause pain, and offer
a sincere apology. We may also feel we can explain to the person
what was going on with us at the time or tell them how we came to
realize that we hurt them. The most important parts of this kind

of conversation are to take responsibility for our actions and to apologize. Hopefully, the other person will accept the apology and we can move on. If there is anything we can do to help the person break free from the impact of what we have done, we can make ourselves available for that. If not, we can simply pray that God will continue to heal and strengthen him or her.

In situations where hurt has been especially deep, people may not be ready to move on. They may, instead, remind us repeatedly of what we have done and use our admissions and apologies against us. Accusations such as, "The reason I am the way I am is that you hurt me so deeply years ago!" Or, "If you hadn't done what you did to me, I wouldn't have done that!" When we hear such words, we can be tempted to feel guilty or condemned about our past actions.

Once we have confessed our sin to God and received His forgiveness, and we have admitted our faults to those we have hurt and apologized to them, we should no longer carry the guilt of our mistakes or failures. God offers us free and ultimate forgiveness, and when we have that, we can view ourselves as clean, regardless of what other people say to us.

John 3:17 says, "For God did not send his Son into the world to condemn the world, but in order that the world might be saved through him," and Romans 8:1 declares that there is no condemnation for those who belong to Him. No matter what you have done, you can live free, forgiven, and healed in Jesus. The people you have hurt may not be quick to forgive you, but God always will be.

Declare this:

I refuse to continue to carry the weight of blame for my mistakes. I have repented and Jesus has set me free!

37

You Are Beloved

*So we have come to know and to believe the love that God
has for us. God is love, and whoever abides in love abides
in God, and God abides in him.*

1 John 4:16

The greatest happiness and peace in people's lives comes from
knowing they are loved unconditionally, for exactly who they
are, with all their strengths and weaknesses, good points and
not-so-good points. I don't think any human being alive, no matter how wonderful or godly he or she might be, is fully capable
of loving us unconditionally all the time. Only God can love us
that way.

God loves us unconditionally in spite of ourselves, no matter what we do. But He does even more than that; He also calls
us His *beloved* (see Romans 9:25). This is a term of endearment
reserved for someone who is very special to someone else, someone who holds a unique place in another person's heart. It means
to long for, to respect, and to hold in affectionate regard. When I
think of the word *beloved*, I sense that it means to be loved in every

way at every moment in time. Because you are God's beloved, there has never been and never will be even a split-second when you are not perfectly loved.

The enemy will use many different things that will challenge your belief that you are beloved. He may use words other people have spoken against you, situations in which you have been victimized, mistakes, failures, disappointments, and anything else that would damage the way you see yourself or cause you to doubt the truth of what God's Word says about you. Well-known minister and author Henri Nouwen wrote: "Self-rejection is the greatest enemy of the spiritual life because it contradicts the sacred voice that calls us the 'Beloved.'"

To fight self-rejection and all the other things that try to contradict the "sacred voice that calls us the 'Beloved,'" we need to do as the apostle John encourages us in today's Scripture verse: We receive God's love totally by faith, coming to know and believe He loves us. The more we meditate on that and persist in believing, the more established it becomes in our hearts.

When we have been deeply wounded, receiving this love is not always easy. Don't get discouraged if you find yourself struggling to accept it. Just let the desire of your heart be to embrace it more and more. If there are times when you feel like you've failed, just begin again. With God, you can always make a fresh start. Eventually, God's unconditional love for you and your place as His beloved will be deeply rooted in your heart and no one will be able to convince you otherwise, but it takes time.

When we are secure in our place as God's beloved, we are strong and confident. We can step into our destiny and into the great future He has planned for us. I encourage you to say out loud today, "I am God's beloved," as often as you can. The more you say it, the more you will believe it.

Declare this:

I am God's beloved.

38

Wanting God's Will

Pray then like this: "Our Father in heaven, hallowed be your name. Your kingdom come, your will be done, on earth as it is in heaven."

Matthew 6:9–10

I learned early in my Christian walk that the soul of a person is composed of the mind, the will, and the emotions. When we talk about having our soul healed, we are talking about finding healing for the things that have hurt or damaged us in our mind, our will, or our emotions. All three areas are important, but today I want to focus on the will.

The *will* refers to our wants, desires, and choices. When we realize that we want something and then we make the decision to get it, we are exercising our will. When someone wants us to do something and we refuse, that is also a choice of the will. If we are going to be healed in our soul, we need to submit and surrender our will to God. We should desire God's will—what *He* wants for us—more than we want our own.

Want God's will with all of your heart because you love Him and want to please Him. Submitting to God's will shows that we trust Him and are confident that what He wants for us is much better than what we want for ourselves. I say, "Pray for what you want and joyfully receive what you are given."

When we seek God's will about various things in life, we do not always find our specific situation in Scripture. The Bible does not tell us whether or not to move to a certain city, whether or not to take a certain job, whether or not to buy a new car, or what we should do about marrying a certain person. It does, however, give us general guidelines that will help us follow God's will. For example, if we are considering whether to make a geographic move or whether to take a certain job, Proverbs 11:14 says, "Where there is no guidance, a people falls, but in an abundance of counselors there is safety." If we pray and seek godly counsel, God may reveal His will through other people, or He may guide us by the presence or absence of peace. If we're thinking about a purchase, the Bible talks about handling money and tells us to be careful with our money (Luke 14:28; Rom. 13:8). When we contemplate marriage, we can find many Scriptures to help us know the type of person we should consider (2 Cor. 6:14; Matt. 19:4–6; Eph. 5:33). We can always count on God's Word and His Spirit to lead us to His will. Sometimes we need to take a step of faith and see if God opens a door we can go through, or if we need to step back and try something else.

When God sees that we want His will more than anything else, He is faithful to reveal it to us. As we walk in His will, we will find that it is better than anything we could ever want for ourselves.

Declare this:

More than anything else, I want God's will in my life. His plan is always better than mine.

39

Give Your Soul a Rest

So then, there remains a Sabbath rest for the people of God.

Hebrews 4:9

If you have ever had a good, hard workout at the gym, you know how nice it feels to give your body a rest afterward. Your body not only enjoys the rest, it needs it. When your soul has been wounded, just like a body after a workout, it also needs a rest. Thankfully, God promises us rest for our souls in His Word. In Exodus 33:14, God speaks to the Israelites, saying: "My Presence will go with you, and I will give you rest" (NIV).

The psalmist declares: "Truly my soul finds rest in God; my salvation comes from him" (Ps. 62:1 NIV). Interestingly, the psalmist speaks to his soul in Psalm 62:5, saying: "Yes, my soul, find rest in God; my hope comes from him" (NIV) and again in Psalm 116:7: "Return, O my soul, to your rest; for the LORD has dealt bountifully with you." Also in Psalms is a phrase familiar to many people, saying that the Lord restores our souls (23:3). When our soul has a chance to rest, it can be strengthened and restored.

In Matthew 11:28–30, Jesus says: "Come to me, all you who are weary and burdened, and I will give you rest. Take my yoke upon you and learn from me, for I am gentle and humble in heart, and you will find rest for your souls. For my yoke is easy and my burden is light" (NIV). A wounded soul can be a heavy burden, but Jesus invites us to come to Him because He will give our souls the rest they need.

Many people whose souls have been wounded try all kinds of ways to feel better and find peace before they ultimately surrender to God. That can be frustrating and exhausting. Nothing and no one apart from God can ever give our soul the rest it needs.

Hebrews 4:1–3 teaches us that we enter into rest by faith, by believing God. It says: "Therefore, while the promise of entering his rest still stands, let us fear lest any of you should seem to have failed to reach it. For good news came to us just as to them, but the message they heard did not benefit them, because they were not united by faith with those who listened. *For we who have believed enter that rest*" (emphasis mine).

Believing (trusting God) is the only doorway into the rest of God. The more we trust God, the easier life becomes because we find that what we commit to Him, He does take care of. He may not do it on the schedule we have set or in exactly the way we want it done, but He will always take the best possible care of us because of His amazing love for us.

Declare this:

My soul finds rest in God, today and always.

40

You Can Bear Good Fruit, Part 1

*By this my Father is glorified, that you bear much fruit
and so prove to be my disciples.*

John 15:8

When we have experienced great pain in our soul, we can hurt
other people or spread negativity without meaning to do so. The
brokenness that affects our thinking, our choices, and our feelings usually affects the people around us, too. Spiritually speaking, this is called bearing, or producing, "bad fruit." But God calls
us to bear *good* fruit. As the Lord heals our soul, we become more
and more able to bear the fruit He wants us to produce.

God would never ask us to bear or produce anything without
giving us what we need to do it. Jesus has everything needed to
produce good fruit, and when He is in us and we are in Him, by
the power of the Holy Spirit, we have what we need to do anything
He asks us to do.

Galatians 5:22–23 lists the fruit of the Holy Spirit, the good qualities we exhibit because He lives in us. They are "love, joy, peace,
patience, kindness, goodness, faithfulness, gentleness, self-control."

Today and tomorrow, we will look at each of these individually, thinking about how God has put them in us and now expects us to bear their fruit.

- **Love:** God is love (1 John 4:8). When He lives in our hearts, our hearts are filled with love. God first loved us, so we have the ability to love others (1 John 4:19).
- **Joy:** Jesus was a man of joy. Before going to heaven at the end of His earthly ministry, He says to His Father in John 17:13: "But now I am coming to you, and these things I speak in the world, that they may have my joy fulfilled in themselves." Many times in Scripture we are encouraged to rejoice, such as in Philippians 4:4: "Rejoice in the LORD always. Again I will say, rejoice!" (NKJV). Because we trust God, we can rejoice in any situation.
- **Peace:** According to Ephesians 2:14, Jesus is our peace. When He is in us, we have peace. When Jesus went to heaven after His ministry on earth, He left us His peace (John 14:27). This empowers us to remain calm and peaceful in every situation. It is important to believe you have these things; otherwise you will never enjoy and walk in them.
- **Patience:** God is extraordinarily patient and slow to anger, and Scripture teaches us to imitate Him. "The LORD is merciful and gracious, slow to anger and abounding in steadfast love" (Ps. 103:8). "The LORD is slow to anger and great in power" (Nah. 1:3). Paul urges us in Romans 12:12 to "rejoice in hope, be patient in tribulation, be constant in prayer," and in Ephesians 4:2, to act "with patience, bearing with one another in love."

When we receive Jesus as Lord and Savior, He lives in us, and everything that is in Him is now in us by the Holy Spirit. He gives us what He wants us to produce. Even if your life has produced bad fruit in the past, you can produce good fruit from now on as the Holy Spirit leads you and helps you.

Declare this:

I bear the good fruit of love, joy, peace, and patience in my life.

41

You Can Bear Good Fruit, Part 2

*By this my Father is glorified, that you bear much fruit
and so prove to be my disciples.*

John 15:8

The apostle Paul writes that he prays for the Colossians to "walk
in a manner worthy of the LORD, fully pleasing to him: *bearing fruit in every good work* and increasing in the knowledge of
God" (Col. 1:10, emphasis mine). As our souls are healed and we
become stronger, we are better able to bear the fruit He wants us
to produce.

Galatians 5:22–23 lists the fruit of the Holy Spirit: love, joy,
peace, patience, kindness, goodness, faithfulness, gentleness, and
self-control. Yesterday we looked at the first four, and today we
will look at the remaining five of these and consider how God has
put them in us and now wants us to bear their fruit.

- **Kindness:** The psalmist says that God's "lovingkindness is
  better than life" (Ps. 63:3 NKJV), and it is His kindness that
  leads people to repentance (Rom. 2:4). The Bible teaches us
  to "be kind to one another" (Eph. 4:32) and to "put on . . .

kindness" (Col. 3:12). Because Jesus lives in you, the ability to be kind is in you also.

- **Goodness:** The Lord is good! This is repeated often throughout the Bible (Exod. 33:19; 1 Chron. 16:34; Pss. 106:1, 107:1, 119:68). The psalmist encourages us to "taste and see that the LORD is good!" (Ps. 34:8). He also praises God by saying, "Oh, how abundant is your goodness, which you have stored up for those who fear you" (Ps. 31:19). The apostle Paul urges us: "Let love be genuine. Abhor what is evil; hold fast to what is good" (Rom. 12:9). The best way I know to enjoy each day is to commit to being good to all people everywhere you go.

- **Gentleness:** The Scriptures compare Jesus to a lamb, which is a very gentle animal. In 2 Corinthians 10:1, Paul appeals to the Corinthians "by the meekness and gentleness of Christ." He also writes: "So, as God's own chosen people,...put on a heart of compassion, kindness, humility, gentleness, and patience" (Col. 3:12 AMP), and "Let your gentleness be known to all" (Phil. 4:5 NKJV).

- **Faithfulness:** He who calls you is faithful. When God's presence passed before Moses, God said this about Himself, "The LORD, the LORD, a God merciful and gracious, slow to anger, and abounding in steadfast love and faithfulness" (Exod. 34:6). Scripture teaches us: "Let not steadfast love and faithfulness forsake you" (Prov. 3:3), and "Only fear the LORD and serve him faithfully with all your heart" (1 Sam. 12:24).

- **Self-Control:** Throughout God's Word, God withholds anger. Proverbs 16:32 says that a patient person is better than a strong warrior, and that someone with self-control is better "than one who takes a city" (NIV). Some people say, "I just don't have any self-control," but if they have received Jesus into their heart, that statement is inaccurate. They do have self-control and simply need to keep exercising it and watch it get stronger and stronger.

As a believer in Christ, you can be confident that everything that is in Him is in you. Believing this truth is the beginning of a new way of living. We don't have to struggle as we try in the flesh to produce these things, but we believe we have them and let each one flow as needed.

Declare this:

My life bears the good fruit of kindness, goodness, gentleness, faithfulness, and self-control.

42

Leave the Wilderness Behind

The LORD our God said to us in Horeb, "You have stayed long enough at this mountain. Turn and take your journey."

Deuteronomy 1:6–7

The Israelites spent forty years making a journey that should have taken them only eleven days. They kept going around and around the same old mountains, but never making any progress. Do you ever feel like you are doing that? Do you keep coming up against the same problems over and over and just don't seem to know how to get past them? In Horeb, God had spoken to them: "You have stayed long enough at this mountain. Turn and take your journey" (Deut. 1:6–7). Then He went on to say, "See, I have set the land before you. Go in and take possession of the land that the LORD swore to your fathers" (Deut. 1:8). I think God is telling us that it is time to press forward and start enjoying the good life He has for us.

One thing that can happen when our soul is wounded is that we can get stuck in life. We can become discouraged about ourselves and about the future. We can easily end up simply trying to survive each day. But that is not the way God wants us to think! He wants us to think about the fact that He wants to heal us and make us strong and whole—and that He has great plans for our future. He wants you to be full of hope, expecting good things to happen to you.

The truth is that God always has new and better things ahead for you. The reason the Israelites made no progress for so long is that they had what I call a "wilderness mentality"—certain mind-sets and ways of thinking that kept them from moving into God's promises and the future He had for them. Examples of the kind of wilderness mentality you might struggle with include: "God loves everyone else more than He loves me." "My past will always be a problem for me." Or, "My dreams will never come true." Any negative, doubt-filled thoughts in your mind will keep you stuck right where you are.

Have you "stayed long enough" at a certain place in your life? Maybe it is a place of abuse or betrayal or deep disappointment. It could be anything that has caused you to feel like you can't move forward or like your life is going nowhere.

It's time to renew your mind according to God's Word (Rom. 12:2) and make a decision to choose your thoughts carefully. Think in ways that agree with God's Word, which says His plans for you are good and will give you hope for your future (Jer. 29:11). Let me encourage you to decide today that you have stayed long enough in the same place. Take God's advice to the Israelites, and "turn and take your journey." Leave your wilderness and wilderness mentalities behind and move toward the great things God has ahead for you.

Declare this:

God has great things ahead for me!

43

No Longer a Victim

He gives power to the weak, and to those who have no might
He increases strength.

Isaiah 40:29 NKJV

Do these words sound familiar to you? *Powerless. Defenseless. Helpless. Hopeless.* Maybe they are familiar because they describe ways you have felt in the past or ways you feel right now. Anyone who has been abused, wounded, or victimized may know exactly how these emotions feel.

The good news is that even if these words describe you today, they do not have to define you in the future. When you ask God to heal your soul and you follow as He leads, you move from being powerless to being powerful, from being defenseless to realizing that God is on your side, from being helpless to having the Helper, the Holy Spirit, living in you, and from being hopeless to being filled with hope and faith. As He heals you, you walk out of sorrow into joy and out of weakness into strength. You exchange every negative thing you have suffered for all the good things God has for you.

You are not weak and helpless, and there are things you can do to protect yourself against further hurt and damage to your soul. Choose your companions in life wisely, and confront people who treat you cruelly and disrespectfully.

In some cases, abuse is so severe and abusers are so dangerous that the best course of action is to get away from them. People who abuse others because they are bullies, though, will often back down when confronted. In fact, they typically do not respect people who meekly accept or submit to their bad behavior. Although standing up to them may be difficult at first, it is usually the only way they will stop abusing. Many of them secretly wish someone would challenge them and stand up to them.

When we choose to stand up to people who bully or abuse us, we should do so after praying and seeking God for the right time, the right place, and the way we are to deal with them. We should certainly use wisdom and also decide in advance that we will behave in godly ways, no matter how ungodly the other person may act.

The only way we will know how to handle this kind of situation properly is to rely on God to guide us and to be obedient to what He teaches us. I had to learn to stand up for myself, and although it was difficult to do, it was worth it. I urge you not to give in to the fear that might be trying to hold you back. God will give you the courage and strength to do what He guides you to do.

Declare this:

I am no longer a victim. I will obey God's Word as He leads me to a place of strength.

44

Never Too Late

The steadfast love of the LORD never ceases; his mercies never come to an end; they are new every morning; great is your faithfulness.

Lamentations 3:22–23

When you are on a journey of healing in your soul, there are times when you feel good about it because you are making progress, and there are times when you encounter setbacks and you wonder if you will ever be made whole. Sometimes the enemy tempts you to wonder if God gets frustrated or exasperated with you because you stumble on your way to healing and wholeness. Sometimes he simply plants in your mind that you have gone too far to be healed, that so much has happened that it is too late. Nothing could be farther from the truth. God is unendingly patient with you. He always loves you, always fights for you, and is always on your side, moving you forward into the very best He has for you. It is never too late to ask Him to help you. And when you ask, He answers.

God's love never runs out, no matter what you do. It is possible to frustrate a human being to the point that he or she may back away from you for a while, but God is not like that. He always stays close. Lamentations 3:22 says His steadfast love "*never* ceases" (italics mine). Plenty of people in Scripture struggled for long periods of time and could have lost hope, but God was always there for them. He always redeemed them and used them in spite of their past mistakes. For example:

- Abraham and Sarah were close to *100 years old* when God fulfilled a promise to them and gave them a child. After a lifetime of barrenness for Sarah, I am sure they thought it was too late for them to become parents (Gen. 21:1–7).
- A woman suffered with a bleeding disorder for *twelve years,* but when she touched the hem of Jesus' garment, she was instantly healed (Matt. 9:20).
- A man unable to walk sat beside a pool for *thirty-eight years* hoping for a miracle to restore the use of his legs. Jesus spoke a word of healing to him and he bent over, picked up his bed, and walked—immediately (John 5:1–9).
- Jesus' friend Lazarus was dead in a tomb for *four days*—not just very sick, but actually dead. Jesus went to his tomb, prayed, and called his name—and he walked out (John 11:38–44).

New beginnings and fresh starts are never in short supply with God. It is never too late for Him to heal a broken heart or restore a life that seems damaged beyond repair. No matter how long you have struggled, it is not too late to hope again. You can dust off your dreams and begin to move forward today. New mercies are waiting for you!

Declare this:

It is never too late for God to heal me, restore me, use me, and give me a great future!

45

True Love

So now faith, hope, and love abide, these three; but the greatest of these is love.

1 Corinthians 13:13

Human beings crave love. When a woman's soul has been wounded, that craving for love often takes one of two forms. Some women develop hard or harsh personalities so other people will not want to get close to them. If the wounds in their souls are related to men, they may make firm decisions not to trust men or not to build relationships with men at all. Other women may be excessive in their desires to have a man in their life, to the point that they are willing to enter into a relationship with any man who pays attention to them. Perhaps you know women like this, women who seem to go from one unhealthy relationship to another. Maybe you have even done it yourself. You keep thinking the next man in your life will finally be the "right" one, only to find yourself disappointed.

When a woman has a string of relationships that never satisfy her, two things are usually true. One, she has not yet found her fulfillment in God alone; and two, she has not yet learned what real love is. In order to stop the cycle of craving love, seeking it from a man, and being disappointed, a woman's soul needs to be healed. Part of that healing involves first receiving God's unconditional love and then understanding what it really means to love and be loved by another person.

I want to share some things I hope will help you in your love relationships with other people. Only God can love us perfectly, but 1 Corinthians 13, which is called "the love chapter" of the Bible, helps us understand what real love is. If someone says, "I love you," but isn't demonstrating the attributes of love in this chapter, you might want to think twice before believing that person and going very far in a relationship.

Love is something that can be seen and felt. It is displayed in a variety of ways. When you are trying to decide whether someone loves you, and whether you love that person, you can use the qualities mentioned in 1 Corinthians 13 as a guide. It says that love is patient, kind, not envious, not boastful, and not arrogant or rude. It also does not demand its own way and is not irritable. It does not harbor resentment. Love "does not rejoice at wrongdoing, but rejoices with the truth. Love bears all things, believes all things, hopes all things, endures all things" (1 Cor. 13:6–7). Love helps others; it gives and it is quick to forgive. This requires intentionality and saying no to self regularly.

The basic qualities of love in 1 Corinthians 13 give us plenty to think about when we consider whether we love someone else and whether they love us. Remember, only God can love you perfectly. Other human beings will let us down, but when we know what true love looks like, we can be wise in our relationships.

Declare this:
I walk in love and develop healthy relationships with others.

46

Keep Your Standards High

Daniel became distinguished above all the other high offi-
cials and satraps, because an excellent spirit was in him.
And the king planned to set him over the whole kingdom.

Daniel 6:3

The Old Testament character Daniel was a person of high standards. We know this because in Daniel 1, when the young men
from Jerusalem were taken to Babylon to be trained in the royal
court, they were supposed to eat the rich food and wine the king
provided for them, but Daniel and his friends asked to be exempt.
He felt such delicacies would defile them, and asked for vegetables
and water instead. Daniel could have gotten in trouble for not eating the rich food, but instead God gave him favor with the man in
charge (Dan. 1:5–20).

In Daniel 6, King Darius decreed that everyone in the kingdom had to pray to him and that anybody who prayed to anyone
else would be thrown into a den of hungry lions. Daniel was committed to praying to the God of Israel, and he continued to do so
despite the decree. When the king found out about this, he had no
choice but to send Daniel to the lions' den. But God shut the lions'

mouths, and no harm came to Daniel. The next morning, the king ordered Daniel to be removed from the lions' den. After Daniel emerged unscathed, the king saw that Daniel's God was the true and living God and issued a new decree that everyone had to worship Him. Daniel went on to prosper in the king's service.

Like Daniel, you may be faced with opportunities to compromise your convictions. Sometimes in the process of having your soul healed, you may feel it would just be easier to go back to your old ways instead of moving forward with God. Let me encourage you to be like Daniel and remain faithful and committed to God. The healing of the soul takes time, and every day may not feel like a great victory. But as you stay in God's Word and continue to obey Him, the progress He desires for you will take place. You will be walking toward greater and greater healing every day as you keep your standards high.

The king saw that Daniel was a person of integrity and that "an excellent spirit" was in him. Obviously, he believed strongly in keeping his commitments, promises, and vows, and he was willing to endure discomfort—and even risk his life—to do so. Because of this, he was promoted to a position of great authority and influence. God has put an excellent spirit in you, too, and you can choose to live in excellence every day. The journey to healing isn't always easy, so I encourage you today to make the decision that you will not compromise. We can see from the story of Daniel that those who remain faithful are rewarded. At the right time and in the right ways, God will honor your faithfulness to Him.

Declare this:

I keep my standards high; I fulfill my commitments; and I remain faithful to God.

47

A Life-Changing Choice

Have I not commanded you? Be strong and courageous.
Do not be frightened, and do not be dismayed, for the
*L*ORD *your God is with you wherever you go.*

Joshua 1:9

There was a time in my life when I had many reasons to feel sorry for myself because of the abuse I had endured during my childhood and because of other things that had happened to me. You may be in that same position right now and be able to think of many reasons to feel sorry for yourself. But I have to tell you that self-pity was a roadblock on my journey to the healing of my soul. It was such a hindrance to me that I devoted an entire chapter to this topic in *Healing the Soul of a Woman*. If you struggle with self-pity, you might find that chapter very helpful.

Self-pity is not something that will go away by itself. We can only break free from it as we refuse to give in to it. After I had struggled with it for a very long time, God spoke to me in a way that changed my life from that moment on. He said, "You can be pitiful or you can be powerful, but you can't be both. Which one will you choose?"

I had been pitiful for long enough, so I chose powerful. But that doesn't mean I *felt* powerful immediately. It simply means I made the choice and decided to let God lead me out of self-pity and into experiencing His power in my life. I hope you will make that choice today, if you haven't made it already.

The first step toward letting go of one way of feeling and embracing another is to see what God's Word says about how you have chosen to feel and who you want to be. Here are some Scriptures that affirm how powerful you are in Christ. I encourage you to read them and meditate on them. Get them into your heart and mind, and they will begin to change you:

- "The wicked flee when no one pursues, but the righteous are bold as a lion" (Prov. 28:1).
- "God has not given us a spirit of fear, but of power and of love and of a sound mind" (2 Tim. 1:7 NKJV).
- "You will receive power when the Holy Spirit has come upon you" (Acts 1:8).
- "On the day I called, you answered me; my strength of soul you increased" (Ps. 138:3).
- "Since we have such a hope, we are very bold" (2 Cor. 3:12).
- "His divine power has granted to us all things that pertain to life and godliness, through the knowledge of him who called us to his own glory and excellence" (2 Pet. 1:3).
- "Fear not, for I am with you; be not dismayed, for I am your

God; I will strengthen you, I will help you, I will uphold you with my righteous right hand" (Isa. 41:10).

- "I can do all things through him who strengthens me" (Phil. 4:13).

Declare this:

I refuse to feel pitiful anymore. I am powerful in God!

48

A Healthy Self-Image

The LORD turned to him [Gideon] and said, "Go in this might of yours and save Israel from the hand of Midian; do not I send you?" And he said to him, "Please, Lord, how can I save Israel? Behold, my clan is the weakest in Manasseh, and I am the least in my father's house."

Judges 6:14–15

People who have been hurt or abused in some way often have very low self-esteem. Other people have not treated them as though they are valuable or special, so they do not have a strong sense of self-worth. An important part of the healing of the soul is developing a healthy self-image and coming to understand that God loves us, so we should love ourselves. We were worth His sending His Son to die for us, so we have worth far beyond what we realize.

In the Bible, Gideon did not have a good self-image. When God called him to save the Israelites and even asked, "Do not I send you?" (which was God's way of letting Gideon know that yes, He was definitely sending him), Gideon tried to get out of it. He basically told God that he did not come from a strong family and that he was the weakest one of them all!

God had chosen Gideon for a special purpose, but Gideon did not have enough confidence in God or in himself to embrace the assignment. He had several problems. The first was that he *thought* negatively about himself. The second was that he *spoke* negatively about himself. The third was that his faith in God did not outweigh his own thoughts and words. Even when we think or speak negatively about ourselves, when we have an encounter with God, it gives us a chance to change our minds, change our words, and come into agreement with Him. Gideon didn't do that.

As God heals your soul, your self-esteem will improve. You will begin to feel stronger, more confident, and better about who you are. This is a good sign, and it means that God is working in your life! When God calls you to do something or gives you an opportunity and your first thought is, *Oh, I couldn't do that. I am not smart enough or strong enough*, or whatever you think you are not enough of, stop yourself. Interrupt that thought and think, *God created me, and He loves me unconditionally. He is healing my soul and making me stronger. I belong to Him, so I can do anything He asks me to do!*

This kind of confidence and positive self-image is not arrogant, because it is based on your relationship with God, not on your human abilities. To be confident in God and to feel good about how He has created you is a healthy expression of your faith in Him. Philippians 4:13 says you can do all things through Christ, who gives you strength. To believe that is to agree with God's Word, and doing that will help you improve your self-image.

Declare this:

I can do all things through Christ!

49

When You Feel Like Nothing Is Working

Then he said to me, "This is the word of the Lord to Zerub-babel: Not by might, nor by power, but by my Spirit, says the Lord of hosts."

Zechariah 4:6

There are times when our soul is in so much pain that we will try anything to feel better. We will read books, attend conferences or seminars, seek counseling, ask for advice from trusted friends, and pursue other things we think will help us. And then we reach the point where we have to admit that nothing is working. We are using a lot of energy, but we are not getting the results we hope for. I can write about this because I have done it, and perhaps you have, too.

I finally realized that many times I was trying to "fix" myself or solve my own problems alone, in my own strength. I was relying on myself and on my own efforts instead of trusting God completely to do what needed to be done. We do have a responsibility to do what we can do and what God leads us to do, but many times we try to go beyond our God-given responsibility. Part of spiritual maturity is realizing that there are certain things only God can do. No amount of effort on our part will do any good, and we will only end up frustrated.

Zechariah 4:6 is the perfect verse we need to remember when we are wearing ourselves out trying to accomplish something only God can do. It is not by human might or power, but only by God's Spirit that certain things will happen. Our job is to trust that He knows what to do and will do it at the right time. Our part is to believe God's promises, and that's why we are called "believers."

Consider these three verses about the Holy Spirit. Jesus says in John 14:26, "The Helper, the Holy Spirit, whom the Father will send in my name, he will teach you all things and bring to your remembrance all that I have said to you." Paul writes in Romans 8:26, "Likewise the Spirit helps us in our weakness. For we do not know what to pray for as we ought, but the Spirit himself intercedes for us with groanings too deep for words." Paul also writes in Acts 1:8, "You will receive power when the Holy Spirit has come upon you."

From these verses we learn that the Holy Spirit helps us, teaches us, ministers to us in our weakness, and prays to the Father for us. He also gives us power, so we know that He is very active in our lives! He is aware of everything we need, and He knows exactly how and when to provide it for us. If we will trust Him, we will see Him move on our behalf and do in our lives what we could never do for ourselves.

Declare this:

Whatever needs to happen in my life will happen—not by my power or might, but by God's Spirit.

50

Your Healing Benefits Others

As for you, be strong and do not give up, for your work will be rewarded.

2 Chronicles 15:7 NIV

Anytime a person is wounded in their soul, that woundedness affects other people. It can have an impact on your social life, especially if your pain has caused you not to trust people or not to want to enter into healthy relationships. If you are a wife or a mother, one of the consequences of the hurt from your past is that it can negatively influence your relationships with your husband and your children, unless you let God heal you. It is sad to think about the fact that the pain one person has suffered can ultimately cause pain to others, but that's the truth. However, there is a greater truth in these situations: your healing can also affect the people around you, and it will have a positive impact on them.

I cannot overemphasize the importance of our relationships with other people. Every area of our lives includes relationships of some sort, whether they are on-the-surface acquaintances, deep friendships, or family relationships. All we have to offer to the people around us is what's inside us. If our hearts are filled with pain, anger, fear, rejection, or other negative qualities, that's what we give the people in our lives. If we are filled with peace, love, joy, hope, and other positive attributes, then we can share those good things with them.

I encourage you today to think about your relationships. Is there a steady stream of good things flowing from you to your family, friends, neighbors, and coworkers? Or do people feel they have to be on guard when they are around you because they have learned they will not hear anything from you that will encourage them or lift them up? Do you talk about yourself and your problems excessively, or do you express an interest in how other people are doing? When you hear about something good that has happened for someone else, can you sincerely rejoice with that person, or do you find yourself jealous inside? Every bit of negativity I have mentioned in this paragraph can be eliminated as your soul is healed. God wants to bring you into a great place of healing and wholeness not only for yourself, but so you can be a blessing to the people you care about.

The journey to healing is not always smooth and easy. It will require you to take an honest look at some painful places in your life and allow the Lord to touch and heal them. In those difficult moments, I encourage you to press on and not to give up, remembering that your healing can have a positive impact on lots of people. I did not like to think about how my past woundedness had hurt other people before my soul was healed, but I rejoice now because God is using the healing He has done in my heart to help others. Stay on your healing journey and watch how He will use you!

Declare this:

My healing not only helps me, it also benefits the people around me.

51

God Is Always with You

Where shall I go from your Spirit? Or where shall I flee from your presence? If I ascend to heaven, you are there! If I make my bed in Sheol, you are there! If I take the wings of the morning and dwell in the uttermost parts of the sea, even there your hand shall lead me, and your right hand shall hold me.

Psalm 139:7–10

A deep wound in the soul influences the way we think about ourselves, the way we perceive others, and the way we relate to God. When we have been very hurt, we can develop a poor self-image and fall into self-rejection. We may also feel that other people are rejecting us (even when they aren't). At times, we may tell ourselves that God is not interested in us or has forgotten about us. That is exactly what the enemy wants us to think, and it is the opposite of what God wants us to believe.

God wants us to know that He loves us unconditionally—no matter how we have failed, no matter how much pain we are in, no matter what other people have done to us or what we may have done to ourselves. We can always go to Him just as we are and not be afraid that He will judge, criticize, or reject us. We can count on Him to deal with us lovingly and mercifully.

The devil wants to use our pain to drive us away from God, but we should choose to let it drive us deeper into Him instead. The devil tries to tell us God is the source of our pain, but in reality He is the only one who can heal us. The Word of God never promises a pain-free life or a life without disappointments and challenges, but it does guarantee that God is always with us (Josh. 1:5), that He never fails us or forsakes us (Heb. 13:5), that He fights our battles for us if we let Him (2 Chron. 20:17), and that He will use our pain and difficulties for good (Rom. 8:28). I have said many times, "Your worst day with Jesus will be better than your best day without Him ever was!"

God spoke to His people through the prophet Isaiah, "Behold, I have engraved you on the palms of my hands; your walls are continually before me" (Isa. 49:16). Think about this. If you were to write a note on your hand, you would see it often and that would keep it on your mind. God says He has engraved you on the palms of His hands. He cannot forget you. He *will* not forget you. To put it another way, you cannot get away from Him or from His love.

No matter how the enemy tries to convince you that God does not care about you, remember that today's Scripture says there is nowhere you can go that God is not there, and Isaiah 49:16 promises He is always thinking about you.

Declare this:

God is always with me, no matter what!

52

Big Things Come from Little Things

His master said to him, "Well done, good and faithful ser-
vant. You have been faithful over a little; I will set you
over much. Enter into the joy of your master."

Matthew 25:23

When I look back on the early days of my ministry, I remember well when the organization was "little," so to speak. Those days required a lot of faith because they were not easy. When I first started doing conferences, they drew only a handful of people, maybe fifty at the most. But the preparation involved in preaching to fifty takes as much time and energy as preparing to preach to five thousand. I had to invest the same amount, but the impact was not as widespread as it is today. Eventually they grew, but I had to be faithful when they were little.

The first van we bought to take our ministry team and equipment to speaking events cost $1,600, and had bald tires and rust spots on it. During those trips, we did not have enough money to spend the night in a motel, so we drove home at night after the evening services had ended, usually arriving about three in the morning. Those were our days of small beginnings, and though they were frustrating at the time, I now know they were very valuable times of preparation for the ministry we have today.

When God heals your soul, you sometimes feel it is happening in very small ways and taking a long time. This is because He is doing deep and thorough work. He is carefully building in your mind, will, and emotions a foundation for strength and wholeness for the days to come. Just as you would want a homebuilder to take proper time and care to lay the foundation of your house, laying a foundation for your future in your soul also takes time and is accomplished little by little.

As your soul heals, I encourage you to pay attention to the little things that happen. You may realize one day that you are not as quick to become angry or fearful as you once were. You may finish a conversation with someone and think, *A year ago that comment would have really hurt my feelings, but today I know that my friend didn't mean it the way it sounded.* You may discover one day that you are willing to stand up for yourself for the first time and are no longer willing to put up with verbal abuse or some other kind of bad treatment. You may find yourself willing to forgive someone you have not wanted to forgive or to begin to trust someone you have been reluctant to trust. All of these things are important to the healing of your soul and they are making you stronger. They may not represent the total breakthrough you are longing for, but they are moving you toward it!

Declare this:

I rejoice in the little things God is doing to heal my soul, and I believe they will lead to bigger things in the future.

53

Boundaries, Not Walls

*Divide this land for an inheritance to the nine tribes and
half the tribe of Manasseh.*

Joshua 13:7

One of the first things God did after the Israelites entered the
Promised Land was tell Joshua to divide the land that still
remained to be conquered among the tribes of Israel. Joshua 13:8–
33 details the boundaries of each tribe, except for the tribe of Levi
because God Himself was their inheritance (v. 33).

Throughout the Bible, God told people and nations what their
geographic boundaries were. As long as different groups respected
the boundaries, they could live peaceably together. But when one
group crossed a boundary and infringed on a neighbor's land,
that's when trouble—and even war—broke out.

Just as groups of people need boundaries, it's also important
for us to have boundaries. Because everyone who wants to come
into our lives may not be good for us, we can decide whether to
allow them to get close to us or not. This kind of boundary setting
can be physical, but it can also be emotional and mental. We get
to decide whether or not we will give certain people access to our

hearts and minds. We can choose how much we will allow our hearts to love or trust them—if at all. We can also choose how much we will think about them. One of the keys to being a healthy individual is to have appropriate boundaries in relationships.

There is a difference between boundaries and walls, and sometimes when a person is very wounded in her soul, she puts up walls instead of setting boundaries. Let me explain the difference. A person who puts up walls says to herself: "I've been hurt before and nobody is ever going to hurt me again! I am not going to allow anyone to get close to me ever again. That way they can't hurt me."

A person who sets healthy boundaries says: "I have experienced a lot of hurt in my life, and I need to protect myself and be involved with people who are safe for me. I am going to be wise and discerning as I build relationships. If someone begins to disrespect me or take advantage of me, I will confront his or her behavior. If it continues, I will not continue to allow the person in my life."

Do you see the difference between building walls and setting boundaries? Building walls leaves no room for healthy relationships because it closes off the possibility of close relationships completely. A person who sets boundaries is open to deep relationships, but only if they are respectful and beneficial. A person with boundaries doesn't shut out all people or certain categories of people, but remains open to people as long as they are positive, not negative, in her life. Setting boundaries is not easy, but God will help you do it.

Declare this:

I no longer close myself off to others by putting up walls. I set healthy boundaries.

54

The Power of Praying for Your Enemies

"I say to you, Love your enemies and pray for those who persecute you, so that you may be sons of your Father who is in heaven."

Matthew 5:44–45

When we think about our enemies, or the people who have hurt us, we often want to run as far away from them as possible. We don't want to see them or think about them. We definitely do not want to love them or pray for them. We simply want to heal from the hurt that is associated with them in our hearts. If we were to follow our feelings, we probably would not ever pray for our enemies, but that is exactly what the Word of God says for us to do. Forgiveness isn't a feeling; it's a choice we make because we want to obey God's Word, and it promotes healing in our soul.

I want to be sure you understand what I mean—and don't mean—about forgiving people. To forgive does not mean that we allow them to continue to treat us badly or that we never confront their bad behavior. Nor does forgiveness mean we let people get away with walking all over us or taking advantage of us. Forgiving our enemies means choosing not to continue to be angry toward them because of what they have done to us and not mistreating them even though they have mistreated us. To forgive means we decide to let God deal with them however He sees fit and we choose not to execute our own type of revenge against them. It also means we will pray that things go well for them, and even pity them because we know they hurt themselves by mistreating others like they hurt us. When they hurt our feelings, God is always ready to heal our hearts.

I believe one reason some people struggle so much with forgiveness is that they fail to pray for their enemies; yet praying for them is a vital step toward truly being able to forgive and ultimately being able to heal. Maybe they don't know how. If you are wondering exactly how to pray for people who have done wrong to you, here are three simple suggestions:

- Pray that they will know God in a personal way.
- Pray that God will reveal anything they need to see about their behavior and how it has hurt others.
- Ask God to bless them.

In addition, you can help yourself heal by not speaking badly about people who have offended you. If you need to talk about it as part of your healing journey, talk to someone who has the ability to truly help you and who will keep it confidential, not someone who will just feel sorry for you, join you in your pain, or spread gossip.

Declare this:

I choose to obey God's Word and forgive and pray for those who have hurt me.

55

Dealing with Anger Appropriately

Be angry and do not sin; do not let the sun go down on your anger, and give no opportunity to the devil.

Ephesians 4:26–27

Anyone who has ever been wounded in her soul knows that anger often results from being deeply hurt. At first we just feel hurt, but then we become angry. We become angry about situations we did not want or deserve, and we become angry with the people who hurt us. When someone abuses or violates us, anger is an understandable and appropriate response. While being angry in itself is not a sin, and there is such a thing as "righteous anger," anger is an emotion that can lead us into sin if we do not handle it properly by confessing it to God, asking Him to help us with it, and forgiving the people who treated us badly. The apostle Paul said we are to be angry and not sin by not letting the sun go down on our anger (Eph. 4:26).

If we insist on staying angry, we will eventually become bitter. Anger and bitterness are both destructive to the soul. The Roman philosopher Seneca must have known this because he said: "Anger, if not restrained, is frequently more hurtful to us than the injury that provoked it."

Many times, we fool ourselves into thinking we are hurting other people by being angry with them, but that is not true. Sometimes they do not even know or care how we feel. Our anger doesn't wound them, but it acts like a poison in our soul, killing our peace and our ability to enjoy life. Anger also affects our ability to think clearly and to make healthy decisions. When we are angry, we can make a lot of bad decisions and display a lot of bad behavior.

Today, I encourage you to study these verses about anger and to ask God to help you handle your anger in appropriate ways:

- "My dear brothers and sisters, take note of this: Everyone should be quick to listen, slow to speak and slow to become angry, because human anger does not produce the righteousness that God desires" (James 1:19–20 NIV).
- "Refrain from anger and turn from wrath; do not fret—it leads only to evil" (Ps. 37:8 NIV).
- "A soft answer turns away wrath, but a harsh word stirs up anger" (Prov. 15:1).
- "Whoever is slow to anger has great understanding, but he who has a hasty temper exalts folly" (Prov. 14:29).
- "Good sense makes one slow to anger, and it is his glory to overlook an offense" (Prov. 19:11).
- "Be not quick in your spirit to become angry, for anger lodges in the heart of fools" (Eccles. 7:9).

- "Let all bitterness and wrath and anger and clamor and slander be put away from you, along with all malice. Be kind to one another, tenderhearted, forgiving one another, as God in Christ forgave you" (Eph. 4:31–32).

Declare this:

I handle anger in a biblical way, according to the Word of God.

56

No Evidence

Then Nebuchadnezzar approached the door of the blazing furnace and said, "Shadrach, Meshach, and Abed-nego, servants of the Most High God, come out [of there]! Come here!" Then Shadrach, Meshach, and Abed-nego came out of the midst of the fire. The satraps, the prefects, the governors and the king's counselors gathered around them and saw that in regard to these men the fire had no effect on their bodies— their hair was not singed, their clothes were not scorched or damaged, even the smell of smoke was not on them.

Daniel 3:26–27 AMP

God's healing work in a person's heart is amazing. When you begin the journey toward healing, many times emotions are raw and raging. The pain in your soul can be so heavy and intense that you wonder if you can even get through the day. Sometimes the pain is so obvious to you that you think other people can see or sense it. You cannot "shake it off" or get away from it. If you want to move forward, you can either suppress it, which is not healthy and will only lead to more problems, or you can seek healing.

When God heals your soul, He heals it completely. You may

remember that something very painful happened to you. You may even remember some of the details of the situation, but when you think about it, it will not still sting. You will be more objective about it and less subjective. In other words, you will know that it happened, but the weight of the personal pain and offense you felt before will be gone. That may be hard to believe, but it's true.

In the Old Testament, King Nebuchadnezzar decreed that everyone in his kingdom should worship a golden idol. If they did not, they would be thrown into a fiery furnace. Three Jewish men, Shadrach, Meshach, and Abed-nego, refused because they were loyal to the God of Israel, so they were thrown into the blazing fire. They should have been incinerated immediately, but they weren't. They survived and came out of the furnace. Daniel 3:27 says, "The fire had no effect on their bodies…even the smell of smoke was not on them." They were definitely in the furnace, but God protected them and delivered them. They suffered no negative consequences from that terrible situation. We might say God healed them completely. He brought them out—strong and whole—from something designed to kill them.

When something hurtful happens in your life, you may think for a while that the pain will never go away. You may believe the negative consequences of that situation will haunt you or influence you for the rest of your life. But as you walk with God, He will heal it completely. You will know that you went through a fire, so to speak, but you will not even smell like smoke. That means you will be completely whole and healed.

Declare this:

God is healing my soul and removing every piece of evidence of the pain I have felt.

57

Trust God with the Heavy Loads

Cast your burden on the Lord [releasing the weight of it]
and He will sustain you; He will never allow the [consis-
tently] righteous to be moved (made to slip, fall, or fail).

Psalm 55:22 AMPC

Today's Bible verse talks about casting our burden on the Lord, which is another way of communicating the idea of trusting Him. Trusting other people is not always easy when our soul has been wounded. At times, trusting God isn't easy either. But God will never let us down. He is the only being in the universe who is completely trustworthy all the time, no matter what. We cannot trust or depend on anyone else 100 percent of the time, but we can always trust and depend on Him.

We understand that we should trust Him, but how do we know that we are doing it? I believe we can be confident that we are trusting God and casting our burdens on Him when we are at rest in our soul. Notice that the Amplified Classic translation of Psalm 55:22 indicates that casting our burden on God means "releasing the weight of it." When you read those words, you can sense the peace of not having to carry a heavy load in your heart or mind anymore, but simply giving it to God and resting in the fact that He will take care of you. He is always faithful.

If we say we are trusting God, but then continue to go through every day worrying about our problems or trying to bear our burdens alone, then we have not released the weight of them completely. Releasing the weight of our cares and trusting God completely requires a decision to surrender the situation to Him, then not to worry about it, try to figure it out, or feel the anxiety of it anymore.

If a problem is weighing on your mind or a situation is heavy on your heart, then you are carrying it. Think of a little child trying to carry something heavy and struggling to lift it or move it. Then think of a father who comes along and lifts it and moves it easily. The reason is that the father is strong and capable of carrying the load, but the child isn't old enough or strong enough yet. The child is so relieved when the father does the job because then he or she does not have to think about it anymore. It's done. The child can rest and enjoy life.

The same principle applies to our relationship with God. He is our Father, and if we will simply put down the burdens we are trying to carry and release them to Him, He will handle them for us. We can rest in Him. We don't have to think about them anymore and can rest in His love for us and in His ability to do exactly what needs to be done in our lives.

Declare this:

I release the weight of my burdens to the Lord, and I trust Him completely.

58

Discover and Use Your Gifts

Before I formed you in the womb I knew you, and before you were born I consecrated you.

Jeremiah 1:5

One of the things that happens as God heals your soul is that you begin to see yourself as He sees you. You receive His love in new ways, and you realize that He has made you special and that He has a unique purpose for your life. God has gifted you to fulfill His purpose for your life, but if you are like a lot of people, you may not have recognized your gifts. When we are in pain in our soul, sometimes all we can focus on is what seems wrong about us. It can be difficult to see what is good and right about us. As God begins to heal our mind, will, and emotions, we find it easier to think about positive things and even recognize positive aspects of ourselves.

I encourage you to start asking God to show you something special about the way He has made you. To some people, He has given a very tender, compassionate heart. Some He has made able to lead others effectively, while others He has created to be excellent followers. Some can cook, some can sew, and some cannot do those things, but they can do other things. To some, He has given a gift of being able to communicate clearly, to teach, to make scientific discoveries, or to write beautiful music. Only you can discover all the ways He has made you unique as an individual.

Romans 12:6–8 talks about giving ourselves to our gifts. In other words, we are to find out what things we are good at and then devote ourselves wholeheartedly to exercising those gifts.

People usually enjoy doing what they are gifted to do. Some people feel they are not good at anything, but that is not true. When we make an effort to do what others are good at doing, we often fail because we are not gifted for those things; but that does not mean we are good for nothing. We should look for what we are good at and do that. As we do what God has created and gifted us to do, we find joy and fulfillment in life.

People who are secure and confident in God know that God has created them to be unique and that they have a special purpose. They realize that He loves them and has a plan for them, and they see no need to compare themselves to others, which is very freeing. I encourage you to be secure enough to enjoy what other people can do and to enjoy what you can do, but never try to be anyone except yourself. Say positive things about yourself instead of negative things because that will help release the gifts God has placed in you.

Declare this:

I will make the most of the special gifts God has given me.

59

Give Thanks in Every Situation

Do not be anxious about anything, but in every situation, by prayer and petition, with thanksgiving, present your requests to God.

Philippians 4:6 NIV

The apostle Paul instructs us to be thankful in every situation, no matter what our circumstances may be. In 1 Thessalonians 5:18, he actually says this is God's will for us. When our soul has been wounded, we do not always feel like being thankful. But Paul says to be thankful "*in every situation*," not just in the situations that are easy or pleasant.

Sometimes all we can do is be thankful that God is getting us through a situation, keeping us and sustaining us each day. We may be on a difficult journey, but we can thank God that He is walking with us every step of the way, that He never leaves us or forsakes us.

The more God heals our soul, the more thankful we can be. Every new level of healing and wholeness we experience is a reason to thank God. But the question is: Can we thank God before we see the big breakthroughs we long for? Can we use our faith to believe He will move in our lives and be grateful for that?

In Exodus 15:20–21, Moses' sister, Miriam, sings a song of praise to God for parting the Red Sea and taking the Israelites through it on dry ground and then putting the waters back together so that Pharaoh and the Egyptians drowned. It is good that Miriam took time to thank and praise God, but anyone can thank Him after He does something great, and it is good to do so. My challenge to you today is to begin to thank and praise Him before you see what you are believing Him for. Don't be like Miriam and merely wait to worship God after you have victory; go ahead and worship Him in advance. This will help you develop a habit of thanksgiving that expresses gratitude to God, regardless of the circumstances.

When Paul teaches us to give thanks "in every situation," he is encouraging us to develop a lifestyle of thanksgiving. We are to thank God throughout each day for everything He does for us, all the ways He helps us, and everything He has promised us. Giving thanks to Him should not be something we do once a day when we sit down to a meal or just before we go to sleep as we try to think of all the good things He has done for us that day. I often say, "Pray your way through the day," as a way of encouraging people to develop a lifestyle of prayer, but it's just as important to thank your way through each day. The more thankful you become, the more aware you are of God's blessings in your life. When you go through life with a growing awareness of His blessings, thanking Him often, every day is easier, happier, and better.

Declare this:

I pray my way through each day, thanking God in every situation.

60

You Are Stronger than You Think You Are

The LORD is my strength and my song, and he has become my salvation; this is my God, and I will praise him.

Exodus 15:2

The devil fills our mind with thoughts such as, *I can't* and *I'm not strong enough*. He wants us to be weak minded so we will give up before we even try. It seems that as we grow from childhood to adulthood, we receive a lot of messages from the world and people that cause us to be afraid that we don't have what it takes. But if you have Jesus, then you have what it takes to do anything He wants you to do. And He definitely wants you to be healed from past wounds and be able to enjoy Him, yourself, other people, and your life.

I encourage you to begin thinking, *I am strong*. The strength I am speaking of comes only from our relationship with God through Jesus. We are not strong in and of ourselves. Jesus said that apart from Him, we can do nothing (John 15:5). Learning to lean on God for all things is one of the first steps to take that will help bring healing and restoration to your soul.

You are stronger than you think you are! My mother confessed to me thirty years after I got away from my father's sexual abuse that she didn't do anything about what he was doing, even though she knew about it, because she didn't think she could face the scandal. My mother thought she was weak and so she was. She stayed with a man who regularly hit her, was unfaithful over and over again, and was abusive and just plain mean. Why? Her own thoughts defeated her. If you have an "I can't" mind-set, or feel that you are simply too weak or not smart enough to do what you need to do, make a decision today to begin thinking strong! Think strong—be strong!

If you see yourself as weak and incapable, you will allow people to mistreat you instead of standing up for yourself. See yourself as the new creation that you are (2 Cor. 5:17), and believe that through Christ you can do whatever you need to do in life. You are far too precious and valuable to allow people to use and abuse you.

We all feel weak at times, but when we do, we can go to God and His Word and draw on His limitless strength. Isaiah said that God never faints or grows weary (Isa. 40:28); that same God dwells in us, and "he who is in you is greater than he who is in the world" (1 John 4:4). Just think about it: The same power that raised Jesus from the dead dwells in us (Romans 8:11).

Declare this:

I am strong and can do what I need to do through Christ, who is my strength.

61

It's Never Too Late to Begin Again

"Remember not the former things, nor consider the things of old. Behold I am doing a new thing."

Isaiah 43:18–19

One of the devil's favorite lies is to tell us that it is too late for us, too many bad things have happened, and no matter what we do, we will never get over it. However, the devil is a liar! When we have thoughts like that, it certainly isn't God putting them in our minds because in Him we can always have hope, an expectation that good is going to happen to us.

Perhaps you tried to begin again and went to a few counseling sessions or went to church with a friend for a couple of months and just gave up because you didn't see any change. If so, don't let that be a reason to think you can't begin again and again and again. God never runs out of fresh starts for His people.

The apostle Paul said that he was determined to let go of what was behind and press toward the goals that God had in mind for him (Phil. 3:13–14). I think Paul did that daily and we should have the same attitude that he did. Each morning is a new day and new chance to start over. When it got dark last night, God pulled down the shades on all our mistakes for that day, and today we begin again!

You may have had false starts at emotional healing, but you are not a failure until you quit trying. God is on your side. He is for you, not against you! I am encouraging you to never give up. No matter how difficult or how slow your healing seems, I urge you to believe that God is still working.

Anyone who has built a successful business or ministry or life has felt like giving up thousands of times, but the difference between them and those who failed is that they felt like giving up but they didn't, while the others felt like giving up and they did.

Everything you have already gone through has taught you some lessons and given you some experience, and it won't be wasted. So even if you did give up for a while, instead of wasting more time feeling guilty, just thank God that you can begin again right where you left off. I wasted a huge amount of time in my life feeling guilty and like a failure, but I hope to help you not make the same mistakes I did. Shake off the guilt and remember that God loves you unconditionally, and His plans for you are always good. When babies are learning to walk, they fall down many times and usually sit and cry for a short while, but then they get up and try again. Eventually they learn to walk, and you will, too.

Declare this:

I forget what is behind and press toward the amazing future God has for me.

62

God Is Just

The LORD is a God of justice; blessed are all those who wait for Him.

Isaiah 30:18 NKJV

The world's way of dealing with people who have hurt us is to try to get revenge. We don't have to look farther than the daily news to hear about someone who has tried to take revenge on another person for some reason. Many times, the person taking revenge is determined not simply to hurt the person who hurt them, but to do something worse.

One of the facts of life is that people will hurt each other. Jesus said, "In this world you will have trouble" (John 16:33 NIV). This means we will be hurt at times and even suffer injustice. But we are not to try to avenge ourselves. Bringing justice is God's job. The apostle Paul writes in Romans 12:19: "Beloved, never avenge yourselves, but leave it to the wrath of God, for it is written, 'Vengeance is mine, I will repay, says the LORD.'"

I have studied the character of God thoroughly, and one aspect of His character that gives me great comfort is the fact that He is just. The simplest way I know to explain this is to say that God will always make wrong things right. I have personally experienced God's justice in many situations. When I am going through something I feel is unjust or unfair to me, I have learned to trust God to make it right in His own way and in His timing. As long as we are trying to get revenge, the person who hurt us is still controlling us, but when we give it to God, we are set free.

Life is not always fair. Sometimes people hurt us in ways that are terribly unjust. If you have ever been completely innocent in a situation and suffered in those circumstances anyway, you know what I mean. If anyone has ever treated you in a way you did not deserve—such as a friend or a family member who hurt you deeply when you had been nothing but good to that person—you also know what I mean. But thank God, He is *always* fair. He understands justice and injustice better than we do, and He sees every wrong thing that happens to us. And He makes it right.

I encourage you today to trust God to bring justice to every injustice that has happened to you. Trusting Him in this way will relieve you completely of feeling you have to somehow take revenge on people who have hurt you. Trusting Him to bring justice means never again wondering how you can get back at someone, or trying to figure out how you can make the person pay for what he or she did to you. Remind yourself often that God is just and that He will bring justice to you. It may not happen the way you envision or as soon as you would like, but He will do it.

Declare this:

I trust in God's ability to bring justice to my life, making every wrong situation right.

Do You Really Want a Quick Fix?

Let patience have its perfect work, that you may be perfect and complete, lacking nothing.

James 1:4 NKJV

When we reach the point that we really want our soul to be healed, we tend to want it quickly. In the natural world, when something breaks, we are happy when it can be fixed fast so we can move on. Just think about it. If your car breaks down, it's disappointing if the repairs cannot be made for three or four days. You want your car fixed right away! Quick fixes, to our way of thinking, are good.

While God is definitely able to give us an instant breakthrough or a miraculous provision, He usually does not work quickly in our lives. More often, He seems to move at a slow pace. This is because He is interested in doing a deep, thorough work in us. He is more concerned with the quality of His dealing with us than with the speed of it. God knows exactly what He wants to produce in us and what He needs to prepare us for, and He is willing to let that process take as long as necessary.

You may be ready for God to fix a situation or do a work in your life before He is ready to do it. If so, resist the temptation to grow frustrated and instead ask God what you can learn from the situation, or how you can grow spiritually while you wait.

Even though you may not be able to tell that anything is changing, remember that God works in the unseen realm. We cannot always see with our natural eyes what He is doing, but He is always working. Your breakthrough may seem to be taking forever, but it is on its way. Instead of focusing on how long you feel you have to wait to see God move in your life, you might try thinking and saying, "God's timing is perfect, and I trust Him. He is working in ways I cannot see!"

Weeds grow quickly, but a large, strong oak tree takes a long time to develop. You could spend every day for a week staring at that oak tree and not see anything happening, but if you wait long enough, you will see it stand tall and mighty. I have heard that slow-growing trees bear the best fruit, and I think that principle applies also to people. The works God does in us over a period of time bear great fruit.

God will never leave you or forsake you (Heb. 13:5). You can count on Him to be actively working in your life, even when the fix you desire does not happen quickly. In those times, stir up your faith to trust His timing and thank Him for His patient care as He does a deep and thorough, excellent quality work in you.

Declare this:

I am patient as I allow God to do a deep work in my heart.

64

Let God Lift Your Head

You, O Lord, are a shield about me, my glory, and the lifter of my head.

Psalm 3:3

In Psalm 3:1–2, we can easily see why David could have been discouraged. An increasing number of enemies were all around him, troubling him. Things were so bad for David that those who were against him said even God could not help him. But David did not dwell on his negative circumstances. Instead, he declared that the Lord was the lifter of his head.

When our soul is wounded, we may feel down in many ways. We may feel down emotionally. We may even physically hang our heads or not stand up straight. Even our eyes and our voices may be lowered. Everything about our being could seem downcast. This happens when we focus on the things that are bad or wrong in our lives instead of following David's example of looking to the Lord.

When we look to God, things start looking up instead of down for us. When we allow Him to lift our heads, we begin to see beyond ourselves. We start to see possibilities and potential instead of problems. We remember that He is bigger than any negative circumstance we face. We can relax in His love, knowing He is taking care of everything that concerns us.

By the end of Psalm 3, over the course of just a few verses, David's attitude has changed completely and he is praising the Lord. In verse 4, he declares his faith that God hears and answers his prayers. That is something you and I can also declare each day, and it will move us from feeling down to looking up.

In verse 5, even though he has said he is surrounded by enemies, he is so confident and at peace in God that he has slept. He rejoices that he wakes up the next day because God sustains him. You and I can learn from this. Even when circumstances are difficult, we can wake up every morning thankful for God's sustaining power and care for us.

In verse 6, David boldly says he will no longer be afraid of the people who have set themselves against him, even thousands of them. Only God could give someone that kind of courage. If God gave it to David, He can give it to you, too.

In verse 7, David prays to be saved from his enemies, and he prays with confidence, knowing God has already given him the victory. God has given you the victory, too, no matter what you are facing.

In verse 8, he praises God for His salvation and asks His blessing on His people. He has moved from despair to worship, and from thinking about his problems to praying for others to be blessed. This is what happens when God lifts our heads!

Declare this:

I praise God because He is the lifter of my head.

65

A Tender Heart

I will give them one heart, and a new spirit I will put within them. I will remove the heart of stone from their flesh and give them a heart of flesh.

Ezekiel 11:19

According to John 10:10, God's desire is for us to enjoy an abundant life—a life of peace, joy, purpose, and above all, love. When we have endured great pain in our soul, our hearts can become hard and unwilling or even unable to love. As Ezekiel 11:19 teaches, it is not God's will for us to be hard-hearted, so we need the Holy Spirit to make our hearts soft and tender again.

People can develop hard hearts for many reasons. I had a hard heart because I had been abused as a child and because people who told me they loved me abandoned me. I can remember a time when I felt that people had used me for their own selfish purposes and taken advantage of me for my whole life. In an effort to try to keep from being hurt any more than I already was, I became hard-hearted.

Once a person's heart becomes hard, making it soft again is

almost impossible to do in human strength. That type of change requires a supernatural work of the Holy Spirit. He is the only One who can reach inside our souls and heal and restore every place of woundedness there. He teaches us about God's love and reminds us that God will never leave us nor turn His back on us (Heb. 13:5).

According to John 16:8, the Holy Spirit also convicts us when we do wrong or mistreat others. When we have hard hearts, we can treat others badly and not care about it. Sometimes we do not even notice it. As the Holy Spirit tenderizes our hearts, we become aware of other people's feelings and begin to care about them. When people's hearts are hard, they can sin against God without feeling bad about it. Sin separates us from God, and part of the way the Holy Spirit draws us back to God is by making us sensitive to our sin so we can repent and return to right relationship with Him.

I do understand how people can become hard-hearted, but I also know that it is a difficult, lonely, miserable way to live. If you have come to recognize hard-heartedness in yourself such as—a general lack of sensitivity toward God and others or a determination not to let anyone get too close to you or not to feel emotion—I encourage you to ask the Holt Spirit to help you. Do not allow yourself to remain in that condition. Ask and allow the Holy Spirit to remove the places in your heart that feel like stone and to give you a heart of flesh that is open, sensitive, and responsive to God and others.

Declare this:

I am open to the work of the Holy Spirit in my heart, making any hard place tender again.

66

It's Time to Stop Pretending

We are his workmanship, created in Christ Jesus for good works, which God prepared beforehand, that we should walk in them.

Ephesians 2:10

People who are broken or wounded in their soul often struggle with identity. They do not really know who they are. In some cases, they have shown people who they are and been rejected, so they decide to try to be someone else instead. People do this by the way they dress, by the way they talk, or by trying to like certain things when they really don't.

For example, think of a high school girl who really loves music and feels most fulfilled when she is playing flute in the band. She is not especially outgoing and does not have a huge group of friends, but she feels comfortable with a small group of others who enjoy making music. But her older sister is popular, outgoing, and athletic—everything she needs to be a cheerleader. Instead of accepting the younger sister and affirming her gift for music, she tells her she will never have dates with the "cool" boys and she will miss out on the best high school parties and social events.

Because the younger sister is not established in her identity, she believes the older sister and tries to change herself to fit in with the cheerleaders.

What is likely to happen to the younger sister? She will not be true to herself, and she will know it. Her band friends may feel she has abandoned them, and the cheerleaders will know she really isn't the cheerleader type, so they will not embrace her. She will end up compromising herself with both groups. More important, she will have betrayed who she is by trying to be someone she is not. This kind of pretending happens all the time—and not just in high school!

Pretending is a form of hiding. By pretending to be someone we are not, we hide who we really are. We think being someone else, instead of our authentic selves, will cause us to be accepted and loved. If we are going to have our souls healed and walk in wholeness, we need to realize that our true identity is not found in what we do, how we dress, how we speak, or what we pretend to like, but we need to know we are accepted, valued, and loved by God and free to be the unique individual He made us to be.

In Ephesians 2:10, the apostle Paul writes that we are God's "workmanship," which means God has created us just the way He wants us to be. We will never have grace to be anyone but who we are. It's time to come out of hiding, stop pretending, and be the person God made us to be. That's the only way we can live the life He wants us to live.

Declare this:

I will no longer pretend to be someone I am not. I embrace the unique person God has made me to be.

67

Trust in God

When I am afraid, I put my trust in you.

Psalm 56:3

God's Word is full of stories about people who trusted in God when they were afraid—and God came through for them. No matter what you're facing today, God will come through for you, too.

When Pharaoh's army closed in on the Israelites at the Red Sea, it looked like they were finished. But Moses, their leader, trusted God, and God performed a miracle. He opened the sea so His people could cross it on dry ground, and when Pharaoh's army followed, He closed the sea again and they all drowned (Exod. 14:5–31). When Daniel was thrown into a den full of hungry lions as punishment for praying to God instead of to the king, God closed their mouths (Dan. 6:7–23). The Bible even says, "Daniel was taken up out of the den, and no kind of harm was found on him, *because he had trusted in his God*" (6:23, emphasis mine). When Jesus' disciples feared for their lives during a storm at sea, Jesus simply spoke to the wind and the waters, and they calmed down (Mark 4:35–39).

You may not be running from an army or tossed on an ocean

right now, but maybe you feel threatened or frightened in some way. Maybe your company is downsizing and you feel threatened financially. Maybe you are afraid of what will happen to your children or grandchildren because of decisions they are making. Maybe fear is trying to control you because of a doctor's report. No matter what the situation, God is bigger than it is. He is able to bring you through it in a miraculous way if you will simply trust Him.

Learning to trust God isn't always easy, especially when we have gone through life feeling that we have to be strong in order simply to survive, or if we have always felt we had to solve our own problems because there hasn't been anyone to help. When we have tried to be in control for years, letting go can be uncomfortable.

Having a relationship with God does not mean we get to do nothing while God does everything. There are definitely times when He moves supernaturally in a situation, but usually He asks us to do something, too. Often, what He asks of us is our trust. He wants us to be willing to stop trying to figure out a circumstance or fix a problem.

What is it that you need to let go of and trust God with? Let me encourage you to begin by saying, "Lord, I trust You with this situation." Once you trust Him, you may be tempted to take it back by going over and over the problem in your mind, by talking about it too much, or by thinking of one more thing you might do to solve it. Resist that kind of reasoning and conversation. Relax, and trust God.

Declare this:
I put my trust in God, and He never fails me.

68

You Have Everything You Need

His divine power has granted to us all things that pertain to life and godliness, through the knowledge of him who called us to his own glory and excellence, by which he has granted to us his precious and very great promises.

2 Peter 1:3–4

The apostle Peter teaches us that God's power provides us with everything we need to live and enjoy a godly life, and He has granted us all of His promises. This means that everything you need for the healing and strengthening of your soul is available to you in Him. Everything you need to live the great life God has planned for you is already yours. You may be wondering how that is possible, especially if you feel like you are still struggling and there is so much you still need.

The way to access what God has provided for you is through the knowledge of God that comes from personal relationship with Him. Growing in personal relationship with Him means taking responsibility for your spiritual maturity through studying God's Word, spending time with Him in prayer and worship, and following the leading of the Holy Spirit. No one can build a relationship with God for you. People can tell you *about* God, but you can only come to know Him in an intimate way if you invest your time and energy in your relationship with Him.

God has provided everything you need through His Son. On the cross, Jesus purchased not only eternal life, but also forgiveness from sin, deliverance, healing, provision, mercy, compassion, hope, power, comfort, peace with God, and countless other benefits. These are powerful, multifaceted gifts. When you are in relationship with Jesus as your Lord and Savior, everything that is His is also yours. You sever yourself from your old life and enter into new life with Him (2 Cor. 5:17). The apostle Paul wrote in Galatians 2:20, "I have been crucified with Christ. It is no longer I who live, but Christ who lives in me. And the life I now live in the flesh I live by faith in the Son of God, who loved me and gave himself for me."

Enjoying a new life in Christ is a process. Little by little, you exchange what you had and who you were for what Jesus offers you and who He is. As you invest time studying God's Word, you are changed into His image from glory to glory (2 Cor. 3:18).

There is nothing you could ever need that Jesus has not purchased with His sacrifice or that God has not provided. Notice that 2 Peter 1:3 says He has "granted to us *all things* that pertain to life and godliness" (italics mine). That means every single thing. Whatever you need today, God has it for you, and you will find it in relationship with Him.

Declare this:

God has given me everything I need for life and godliness.

69

Resisting the Enemy

He shall speak words against the Most High, and shall wear out the saints of the Most High.

Daniel 7:25

One of the many reasons God wants to heal your soul is to make you strong so you can live the life Jesus died to give you and enjoy it. The devil, on the other hand, wants to keep you weak. He knows you will struggle and be frustrated as you attempt to follow God's lead in your life and fulfill His purpose for you if he can keep you weary and worn-out. Daniel 7:25 clearly tells us that one of the enemy's strategies against us is to wear us out, and we would be wise to guard against that happening in our lives.

If you think about how you become worn-out physically, you realize that it happens over a period of time as you become excessive in things like working too much, not getting enough sleep or rest, or even worrying a lot. Many people confess that they feel weary and worn-out, but they don't know how it happened. The enemy works to get you out of balance in your life, but he does it gradually—a little bit here and a little bit there. He does not want to call your attention to what he is doing, so he usually works in ways you may barely notice. He knows it takes more than one attack to wear you out, so he comes against you again and again. And he is relentless. He will send one situation into your life to make you a little tired, then a circumstance that takes a little more out of you, then a series of thoughts about how tired you are. He will attack one area of your life, then another, then another—until you are spiritually worn-out and have lost your energy to fight.

In Deuteronomy 7:22, God tells the Israelites that He will drive their enemies out of their midst "little by little." That's the way for them to gain victory. The enemy also understands that "little by little" is an effective strategy for his purposes. Just as God uses it to give His people victory, the enemy uses it to try to defeat us.

When Satan attacks, we should immediately begin to use our spiritual weapons—praising and worshipping God, praying, and standing on the truth of God's Word. When the enemy speaks lies, we should speak truth. When he tries to separate us from God, we should draw near to Him.

I strongly believe that God is healing your soul for a great purpose and that He wants to use you mightily in His kingdom. But the enemy wants to wear you down so you will never be strong enough to rise up and take the place God has for you. Resist him when he first comes against you, and every time he tries to wear you down, you will have the victory.

Declare this:

I resist the enemy at his onset. I will not allow him to wear me out.

70

No Looking Back

*Jesus said to him, "No one who puts his hand to the plow
and looks back is fit for the kingdom of God."*

Luke 9:62

Part of the beauty of what happens when God heals your soul
is that He offers you a fresh start, a whole new beginning. But
embracing the new life He has for you will be very difficult if you
are still holding on to the past. Think of it very simply. If you are
walking through the grocery store with your hands full of oranges
and someone tries to give you several apples to carry, you cannot
hold them. In order to take the apples, you have to put down the
oranges. That's exactly how it works with the new beginning God
offers you.

Part of freeing yourself from the load of your past means refusing to look back and not replaying certain scenarios in your mind.
Refusing to look back means resisting regret, turning away from
past relationships that are not good for you, and letting go of mistakes and feelings such as guilt and shame.

Paul writes in Philippians 3:13 that he forgets what lies behind
and strains "forward to what lies ahead." It's interesting that Paul

says he strains forward. This tells us that moving ahead requires effort. It may sound exciting, but it's not always easy. Letting go of the past can be hard to do, but it is much better than remaining stuck in it.

When God asks us to let go of the past and look toward a better future, He gives us the grace to do it. We need to be very careful about thinking or saying that what God asks of us is too hard. Nothing is too difficult for Him (Jer. 32:17), and He lives in us by His Spirit (1 Cor. 3:16), who empowers us to do what God wants us to do.

In Genesis 19, a man named Lot and his family lived in a city so filled with sin and perversion that God destroyed it completely. Through some angels, God warned Lot ahead of time and told him to get out of the city with his wife and daughters. But they did not move quickly, so in God's mercy the angels took them by the hand and led them away, saying, "Escape for your life. Do not look back or stop..." (Gen. 19:17). But Lot's wife disobeyed and looked back anyway—and turned into a pillar of salt (Gen. 19:26)! The angels were trying to save her life, and all she had to do was not look back and not stop. She just had to look ahead and keep going forward. But she chose not to do it, and it cost her everything.

Let me encourage you to keep looking ahead and to keep moving forward. God has great things in store for you!

Declare this:

Every day I embrace the new beginning God has for me.

71

Four Powerful Words

Death and life are in the power of the tongue, and those who love it will eat its fruits.

Proverbs 18:21

One way the devil may try to keep you trapped in pain in your soul is by making you think you are missing out on something good you could have enjoyed had you not suffered the way you did. He may try to convince you that your life was destined to be wonderful before those painful events took place, but now that you have been wounded, it will not be as good as it might have been.

This scheme of the enemy usually starts with two words: *If only.* I had to learn to resist thinking and saying "if only" statements, even after I became a Christian. I wasted a lot of time thinking, *Things are better for me now, but they would be even greater if only I had not been abused. I would not have some of the problems I have now if only I had a normal childhood with parents who loved me properly.*

You may be thinking similar thoughts, which could include, *If only my loved one had not gotten sick and passed away, I would be happy.* Or, *It would be so much easier for me to enter into new relationships if only So-and-So had not betrayed my trust and abandoned me.* Maybe even as you are reading this, you can identify an "if only" thought specific to your situation or remember a time when you said, "If only..."

"If only" brings up negative thoughts and emotions and leads to negative confessions, so I want to suggest an alternative. Instead of "if only," what if you were to think and speak the two positive words "but God"? Think for a moment about how that would change the way you see yourself and the way you view your life.

I encourage you today to find a "but God" statement to think about and speak. It could be, *I had a very painful childhood, but God is healing me completely and restoring my soul*, or *I spent many years frightened, worried, and anxious, but God has given me peace, power, love, and a sound mind* (2 Tim. 1:7). It might also be something like, *Because of my past, I have never been able to look forward to the future, but God says He has good plans for me and He gives me hope* (Jer. 29:11).

Proverbs 18:21 teaches us that the tongue is powerful. What we say can lead to life or death. And all of our words begin with our thoughts. I encourage you to watch out for negative thoughts and statements that include "if only," and to think and say instead positive confessions that include "but God." When you focus your thoughts and words on what God can do, His power will flow in your life in unprecedented ways.

Declare this:

I do not think or say, "If only." I think and say, "But God."

72

Serve Others through Prayer

Praying at all times in the Spirit, with all prayer and sup-plication. To that end, keep alert with all perseverance, making supplication for all the saints.

Ephesians 6:18

One of the great temptations we often face when we have been wounded is to think too much about ourselves. We may focus excessively on our pain, on what happened to us, or on what will happen in the future. One of the best things we can do for ourselves is to get our minds off ourselves and think about what we can do for others. We may not have extra resources to bless them in physical ways, but we can always pray for them, and that's called interceding. It doesn't take any money; it doesn't require us to travel to get to them; it doesn't demand anything of us except a willing heart and some time.

When we are hurting, we often see everything in life through a lens of pain. When that happens, we may find ourselves being hard on people instead of being gracious and showing kindness. But judging or criticizing others only holds us in bondage. If we pray for people instead of judging them, interceding for them as frequently and fervently as we pray for our own needs, we will not only be a blessing in their lives, we will also experience the joy of serving others.

In the days of the prophet Ezekiel, God was looking for people who would "stand in the gap" for others (Ezek. 22:30 NKJV). I believe He is still looking for that kind of intercessor today. If there is a gap, or distance, in people's relationship with God for some reason, we have the privilege of praying that their relationship with Him will be restored. If people have needs, we can intercede for them and expect to see them comforted and encouraged while they wait for God to provide for them.

A life focused only on self is a sad, lonely, narrow existence. When we reach out to others and include them in our lives, even in such a simple way as praying for them, we enrich ourselves and reach beyond our own little world. We begin to care about them in new ways; we begin to share their concerns and burdens— and somehow our concerns and burdens seem lighter. We rejoice when God answers our prayers for them. We grow in our faith as we trust God to move in their lives—and soon we realize we have more faith for Him to move in our lives, too.

There are many benefits to serving others through prayer, both for the ones we intercede for and for us. Praying for people strengthens our relationship with God and our relationships with them, which is good and healthy for everyone.

Declare this:

I will not think only of myself. I will think also of others and begin to serve them through prayer.

73

Trust God's Decisions

Oh, the depth of the riches and wisdom and knowledge of God! How unsearchable are his judgments and how inscrutable his ways!

Romans 11:33

"If only this situation would change, I would be happy!" That's what a lot of people say when their souls have been wounded. They are miserable in their pain, and they think if something would just change for them, everything would be better. People suffering the hurt of rejection or abandonment tend to think their lives would improve if they had a good friend, a loving family, or a spouse. People in unhappy marriages sometimes believe things would get better if they could just have a child. Those who live with strife and worry because of a wayward child are convinced things will improve when that child leaves home. People who have been mistreated or abused long for someone to be kind to them because they think that will relieve their pain. Often, we believe the solutions to our problems are in things we want God to give us or do for us. We pray for Him to do these things and become frustrated when He does not.

In the short Book of Jude is a verse we might easily overlook, but it teaches an important lesson about what can happen when someone does not trust God's wisdom and direction: "Woe to them! For they walked in the way of Cain and abandoned themselves for the sake of gain to Balaam's error and perished in Korah's rebellion" (Jude 11).

What did Cain, Balaam, and Korah have in common? All of them tried to get something God was not giving them. Cain was jealous of Abel because Abel had God's approval and Cain wanted it, so he killed him (Gen. 4:3–8). Balaam disobeyed God and chose worldly honor over doing God's will. He then became so deceived that God had to speak to him through his donkey to get his attention (Num. 22:22–31). Korah resented Moses because he wanted the position and power Moses had. His rebellion ended up costing him his life (Num. 16:1–33).

Cain, Balaam, and Korah all sinned in order to try to get something God was not ready to give them. They thought they knew better than God did what they needed and what would make them happy. They all suffered greatly because they did not trust God's wisdom and chose to make their own decisions instead.

I assure you that God is aware of your situation and your struggles. He wants to heal your heart and to fill your life with peace, love, and joy. He knows what you need, how you need it, and when you need it. I encourage you today not to try to make things happen for yourself just because you think they will make you feel better, but to trust His decisions and let Him do what He needs to do in your life in His way and in His timing.

Declare this:

I trust God's decisions for my life, and I will wait for Him.

74

The Greater One Lives in You

He who is in you is greater than he who is in the world.
1 John 4:4

I want to remind you today that God is greater than anything the world or the devil could set against you. Because you are a believer, God lives in you by His Spirit (1 Cor. 3:16). This means you have everything it takes to do what you need to do and to do it with boldness and confidence. You may not know exactly how to do it, but God will teach you. You may not be able to foresee the obstacles you will face, but God will go before you and make your way plain. You may not be able to see the outcome, but as you walk in obedience to Him, God will make sure you accomplish what He has planned. He will guide you and help you every step of the way as you walk by faith. He is always with you.

Because the Spirit of God lives in you, you can do and be much more than you could ever do and be on your own. All the truths in His Word apply to you. I want to mention some of those truths today so you can focus your thoughts on them and get them into your heart.

- You are loved with the never-ending love of God (Jer. 31:3).
- You are accepted unconditionally (Eph. 1:5–6).

- You are forgiven of every sin you have ever committed or will ever commit, and you are cleansed by the blood of Jesus (Eph. 1:7).
- You are God's child (1 Peter 1:23).
- You are healed by Jesus' stripes (Isa. 53:5; 1 Peter 2:24).
- You are redeemed from the curse of sin (Deut. 28:15–16; Gal. 3:13).
- You are strengthened with all power according to God's glorious might (Col. 1:11).
- You are an overcomer by the blood of Jesus and through the word of your testimony (Rev. 12:11).
- You are God's workmanship, created in Christ to do good works that have been planned for you since before you were born (Eph. 2:10).
- You are the righteousness of God in Christ (2 Cor. 5:21).
- You are delivered from the power of darkness and are now part of God's kingdom (Col. 1:13).
- You are more than a conqueror through Jesus, who loves you (Rom. 8:37).
- You are able to do all things through Christ, who gives you strength (Phil. 4:13).

These are just some of the verses that tell you who you are because the greater one lives in you. The Bible includes many more truths. I encourage you to fill your mind with them today and let them guide your life.

Declare this:

The greater One lives in me!

75

God Is Faithful

Know therefore that the LORD your God is God, the faithful God who keeps covenant and steadfast love with those who love him and keep his commandments, to a thousand generations.

Deuteronomy 7:9

Sometimes the reason we are wounded in our soul is because a person we thought we could trust has betrayed us. That can be a very painful experience. Some people, when they have felt let down, cheated on, or betrayed in some way, begin to wonder if they can ever trust anyone again—even God.

I want you to know today that God can be trusted all the time, in every way. Moses wrote in Numbers 23:19, "God is not man, that he should lie, or a son of man, that he should change his mind. Has he said, and will he not do it? Or has he spoken, and will he not fulfill it?" And Jesus said in John 4:24, "God is spirit, and those who worship him must worship in spirit and truth." Both of these Scriptures, one from the Old Testament and one from the New Testament, remind us that God is not a human being, and He does not think, speak, or act like humans do. He is higher and better than any person could ever be. He is incapable of treating us badly or doing us wrong. Everything He does is motivated by love, and He is faithful in every way.

Looking back over my life, I can firmly declare that God is faithful. Even at times when I could not see Him or feel Him, He has been there for me. He is there for you, too. As long as we believe He is working, He will reveal to us at just the right time what He has been doing for us. You may feel like you have to wait for Him for a while, but don't give up. Keep trusting in His faithfulness.

One way I remind myself of God's faithfulness is by looking at various journals I have kept for more than forty years. In them, I record things God has asked me to do, or not to do, and things He has done for me. As I read and remember what God has done for me in the past, I am strengthened to believe He will come through for me again in the present moment and in the future.

I encourage you today to think about times God has been there for you, times He has rescued you, times He has provided for you, and times He has shown you His love. If you have not known Him very long, maybe you would like to do what I have done and start keeping a journal. Begin to write in it what you are trusting God for, and when He comes through for you, write that also. Soon, you will have a record of His faithfulness that you can reread anytime you need to be reminded that He is faithful.

Declare this:

God is a faithful God, and I believe that He is faithful to me in every situation.

Confidence in God

In the fear of the Lord one has strong confidence, and his children will have a refuge.

Proverbs 14:26

As God heals our soul, one thing we notice is that we become stronger and more confident. With every step of healing He leads us through, we see that He is faithful and trustworthy, and this increases our confidence in Him. Life is much easier and more enjoyable when we are confident than it is when we feel hesitant or unsure. When we are confident, we believe and feel certain we can do something, and that belief empowers us to live with courage, joy, and hopeful expectation. A confident woman can look at herself in the mirror each day, no matter what she's facing, and say, "You and God together can do anything you need to do today."

The most important thing about confidence is to know where it comes from. Some people are capable of developing an attitude of confidence in themselves, thinking, *I can do this!* and *I've got what it takes!* But as believers in Jesus, our confidence comes from Him. Anyone can feel confident in certain areas, but we can be confident in all areas of life as we find our confidence in God. He gives us not only confidence in what we can do, but also in who we are. Our ability to be confident comes from the fact that He loves us, He fights our battles for us, He is always leading us to victory, and we belong to Him.

If we put our confidence in ourselves, we will eventually be disappointed. Writing to fellow believers, the apostle Paul declared that we "glory in Christ Jesus and put no confidence in the flesh" (Phil. 3:3). When we trust in God with confidence, we no longer struggle with stress, worry, or fear of what will happen if we don't do everything right.

The Old Testament prophet Jeremiah understood, as Paul did, that we cannot place our confidence in ourselves. He wrote, "Cursed is the one who trusts in man, who draws strength from mere flesh...But blessed is the one who trusts in the Lord, whose confidence is in him" (Jer. 17:5, 7 NIV).

An important point I like to make is that in Christ we can *be* confident even when we do not *feel* confident. We cannot trust our feelings because they can change at a moment's notice and without warning. Instead, we can put our confidence in *Christ*.

God's Word is full of powerful truths we can trust and depend on, truths that will build a firm foundation of confidence in God for our lives. People may cause you to change the way you feel about yourself, especially if they do or say something that undermines your confidence or makes you wonder if you are weak. But no one can change the truth of what God says about you or who He is in your life. So put your confidence in Him!

Declare this:

I have no confidence in my flesh, but I am fully confident in God.

Follow Peace

Let the peace (soul harmony which comes) from Christ
rule (act as umpire continually) in your hearts [deciding
and settling with finality all questions that arise in your
minds, in that peaceful state] to which as [members of
Christ's] one body you were also called [to live]. And be
thankful (appreciative), [giving praise to God always].

Colossians 3:15 AMPC

Colossians 3:15 in the Amplified Bible, Classic Edition, has been
a very important verse to me for a long time. I especially like the
way it presents the peace of Christ as an umpire in our hearts. In
baseball, there are several umpires on the field and their job is
to determine whether players are in or out of the game. Umpires
make the decisions, and they have the final say. If we think of
peace in the same way, we see that we can let it decide what gets to
come into our lives and what needs to get out of our lives.

Peace is a fruit of the Holy Spirit. It is one of God's gifts to those
who trust Him, and one way He leads us is by peace. Near the end
of Colossians 3:15, Paul even writes that as believers we are called
to live in peace.

When our hearts and souls are wounded and in pain, they are not at peace. As God heals us, one thing we notice is that our peace increases. We begin to feel more peaceful on the inside, and we want to do things that give us peace, not things that steal our peace. Let's say God is healing your soul right now from rejection or abandonment in the past. He has strengthened you to the point that you want to build new relationships and learn to trust people again. You may meet someone who seems like he or she would be a wonderful friend, but as you get to know that person, something inside you just feels unsettled. Even though everything on the outside may make the person appear to be someone you would want as a friend, you do not feel peace about continuing to develop the relationship. You would be wise to follow peace and choose another person to become friends with, someone about whom you do feel peace. This same standard of making choices according to whether or not you feel peace applies to any decision in your life.

I am sure that you have numerous decisions to make each day. As you consider your options, look for the one that brings peace to your heart and follow that. At times you may feel that following peace means making a decision that does not make sense to your natural mind. That may be because God sees and knows things you do not, and He is guiding you to make the decision that will be best for you later on.

Declare this:

In every decision I make, I follow peace.

78

Overcoming Self-Doubt

If any of you lacks wisdom, let him ask God, who gives generously to all without reproach, and it will be given him. But let him ask in faith, with no doubting, for the one who doubts is like a wave of the sea that is driven and tossed by the wind.

James 1:5–6

When you need to make a decision, do you worry and feel stressed about which option is right? Or can you evaluate information, make the decision, feel good about it, and move forward without looking back? Once a decision is made, do you wonder if you made the right choice or wish you had done something different? Being excessively indecisive is a sign of self-doubt and can be called being "double-minded." According to James 1:5–8, a double-minded person is like a wind-driven wave and will not be able to receive help from God. The Bible shows us how to overcome self-doubt and double-mindedness.

Some people demonstrate self-doubt when they are faced with decisions and are so afraid of making the wrong one that they won't decide anything at all. They think they can protect themselves from making a mistake. But not making a decision is actually making a decision to not make a decision! Every decision you make will not be the right one, but God can take a wrong decision and still lead you to the right outcome. He can also teach you valuable lessons you might not learn any other way.

Other people struggling to make a decision have the right idea in turning to God's Word, but make the mistake of wishing they could find in the Bible *exactly* what to do in a certain situation. For example, they may want a simple *yes* or *no* for a very specific personal decision they face. To help us make those decisions and overcome self-doubt in various situations, the Bible sets many standards and offers many guidelines.

Below are four decisions you can feel confident about because they are based on God's Word. Knowing your decisions are in agreement with His Word will empower you to stand against self-doubt. Practice making decisions like these, and it will strengthen your ability to make decisions without second-guessing yourself.

- Decide to grow in your study of God's Word and in prayer.
- Decide to believe the best, not the worst, in every situation.
- Decide to focus on what God says about you, not what other people say.
- Decide to be hopeful, not fearful, about your future.

The remedy for self-doubt is confidence. Part of the fruit of the healing of the soul is increased confidence—not in ourselves, but in God. We will not be right about everything all the time, but we will not be wrong about everything either. We need to learn to ask the Holy Spirit to lead us, follow godly wisdom, and then trust God to help us make good decisions.

Declare this:

Because I can trust the Holy Spirit who lives in me, I no longer doubt myself.

79

God Understands

*For we do not have a High Priest Who is unable to under-
stand and sympathize and have a shared feeling with our
weaknesses and infirmities and liability to the assaults
of temptation, but One Who has been tempted in every
respect as we are, yet without sinning*

Hebrews 4:15 AMPC

In Job 4:7–8, Job's friend Eliphaz gives him wrong advice because
he totally misunderstands Job and the cause of his trouble. He says
that he thinks Job has brought his problems on himself. Though
the Bible calls him Job's friend, he is not a very good friend.
Because he does not understand the situation, he cannot offer Job
the support he needs. Job not only has to deal with Eliphaz, he
also has two other friends who do not understand him either.

Sometimes people in our lives are like Job's friends. We hope
and think they will understand and comfort us in our struggles,
but they do not. Sometimes even the people who are the closest to
us do not understand our challenges, our dreams, our personality,
or the call of God on our lives.

Before I realized God was calling me to teach His Word, people misunderstood me and thought I was too serious. They wanted me to do frivolous things with them that did not interest me. I always had a desire to do something that really mattered, I just did not know what it would be.

I now realize that God's call on my life has required me to be serious about many things, to work hard and stay focused. My personality and abilities were what I needed for what God was going to call me to do, but the time to put those things to use simply had not come yet. Sometimes we don't even understand ourselves, but God knows exactly what He is doing and has planned for our future.

As God is healing your soul, strengthening you and preparing you for His use, and as you are discovering what He wants you to do, you might also feel out of place. You may feel that you do not fit with the people around you or that you do not truly belong in some of the situations in which you find yourself. You may be tempted to be confused or bothered when people don't understand you, but the best thing is not to be overly concerned with what people think, but instead to care about what God thinks.

Part of your training to fulfill God's plan for your life is realizing that people will misunderstand you at times, just as they misunderstood Jesus. When that happens, it's important to make up your mind to stand with God and do what He says even if no one understands you, agrees with you, or supports you.

I believe God wants to do great things through you, so stick with Him even when others do not understand. Most often, people who do not support you do not mean to hurt you; they simply do not understand. God always understands, and you can talk to Him anytime.

Declare this:

When people around me misunderstand me or struggle to relate to what I'm going through, God understands me and helps me.

80

Taking Care of Yourself in Relationships

I was your cure, and you were my disease. I was saving you, but you were killing me.

Author unknown

Sometimes the wounds of the soul result from bad choices people around us have made. As God heals your soul, you may notice that certain relationships in your life are changing. You may sense a need for space in a relationship with someone you feel very close to. Or you may have done a lot of things with one person for a long time, but now you are beginning to want to broaden your circle of friends. You may have been someone's "go to" person in every situation, but you are starting to feel he or she is asking too much from you. Different relationships change in different ways, and when God changes you (which is what happens when your soul is healed and strengthened), do not be surprised if some of your relationships need to change, too.

Many people in the world today need help. If we love them, we want to help them and we are often willing to spend time, effort, and money to do whatever we can do for them. The Bible clearly teaches us to love and serve one another (John 13:34; Rom. 13:8; Gal. 5:13). But sometimes we can help people too much, to the point the relationship becomes codependent, which is very unhealthy.

When people are codependent, it means they allow someone else's problems or bad choices to control them. They don't know how their day will go because they wait to see how the other person is, and what he or she needs. If we allow ourselves to be in a codependent relationship, we are enabling another person's bad or unhealthy behavior. We are not truly loving that person or allowing him or her to grow and mature. We are also failing to love ourselves.

When a scribe asked Jesus what was the greatest of all the commandments, Jesus said that the most important is to "love the LORD your God with all your heart and with all your soul and with all your mind and with all your strength" (Mark 12:28–30). Then He went on to say that the second most important commandment is this: "You shall love your neighbor as yourself" (Mark 12:31). Clearly, God wants us to love ourselves—not to be selfish or self-centered, but to love ourselves in healthy ways, just as we love others in healthy ways. He has called us to help people and even to do so when we have to sacrifice something for ourselves, but He has not called us to allow other people's choices to control or manipulate us.

Whenever you see a Bible verse that talks about loving others, apply it also to loving yourself. That will help you be a good friend or family member, while also helping you take care of yourself in relationships.

Declare this:

I am committed to loving other people, while also loving myself.

81

Jesus Is Merciful

*When he heard that it was Jesus of Nazareth, he began to
cry out and say, "Jesus, Son of David, have mercy on me!"*
Mark 10:47

Mark 10:46–52 tells us the story of a man sitting beside a road beg-
ging. The man, named Bartimaeus, was blind, so we might assume
he was unable to work and had to depend on people's kindness to
meet his needs.

One day, Jesus was walking down the road near Bartimaeus and
heard him shouting, "Jesus, Son of David, have mercy on me!" (Mark
10:47). The crowd around Bartimaeus told him to be quiet and stop
bothering Jesus. But Bartimaeus ignored them and kept crying out
anyway. I believe he was determined to have an encounter with God.

Jesus had a choice to make. He could have pretended not to hear
Bartimaeus or He could have simply kept moving without saying anything. But Jesus was merciful, and His mercy was on full
display toward Bartimaeus that day. He stopped and asked some
of His disciples to bring Bartimaeus to Him. When Jesus asked
Bartimaeus what he wanted Him to do for him and Bartimaeus
responded that he wanted his sight restored, Jesus healed him.

I have said many times that mercy precedes healing. Many of us do not cry out for God's mercy enough. There may be various reasons for this, such as feeling unworthy or spending our time trying to earn it, when we can never do so.

When people in the Scriptures found out Jesus was nearby, they went to Him and asked for mercy. Always remember that Jesus is near to you, too. You can ask Him for mercy at any time, under any circumstances, and He will hear your cry. A father whose son was terribly tormented, to the point of hurting himself, asked Jesus for mercy for the young man, and Jesus healed him (Matt. 17:15–18). A woman whose daughter needed deliverance from demonic oppression cried out for mercy (Matt. 15:22–28), and Jesus set her free. Ten men afflicted with the horrible disease of leprosy asked for His mercy, and He healed them all (Luke 17:12–19). As you can imagine, they were so excited, but only one of them thought to go back to Jesus to thank Him.

A word that is similar in meaning to *mercy* is *compassion*. The King James Version of Matthew 9:36 says that as Jesus traveled and ministered, He was "moved with compassion" toward people. In other words, His awareness of people's needs touched His heart. He cared about each one, and His mercy and compassion moved Him to action. His mercy is available for you today.

The Bible says that His mercies are "new every morning" (Lam. 3:22–23). When you need mercy from God, all you have to do is ask. And when He gives it to you, remember to thank Him!

Declare this:

God's mercy is always available to me, and I am thankful for it.

82

The Soul-Body Connection

Bless the LORD, O my soul; and all that is within me, bless His holy name! Bless the LORD, O my soul, and forget not all His benefits: who forgives all your iniquities, who heals all your diseases.

Psalm 103:1–3 NKJV

Have you ever known people who were deeply wounded in their soul and also struggled with problems in other areas of their lives? I can think of many examples of this. The reason it happens is that the soul is not isolated from the rest of our being. Every individual is a three-part being. We are spirit, soul, and body, and each of these components affects the others.

We have heard of the "mind-body connection," but I think we can broaden that a bit and say there is a connection between our soul (which includes the mind, but also includes the emotions and the will) and our body. Emotions definitely affect people physically. Emotions such as anxiety can give people digestive troubles, while anger can lead to elevated blood pressure and headaches. I also believe the will—what we want to do and the choices we make—impacts the physical aspects of our lives. There is no doubt that choosing to eat only junk food, not exercising, and failing to get adequate rest will compromise physical health. Whatever is in our soul works its way out of us through the body. And if we feel bad physically, that will affect our souls also. Likewise, if we have wounds in our souls, they can affect our health (bodies).

Not all physical problems are rooted in the soul, but some of them are. Numerous scientific studies have proven that stress, which affects the soul (mind, will, and emotions), can cause disease. God did not design us to carry stress in our souls that will compromise our bodies. Jesus says in Matthew 11:28–29 that we are to come to Him and find rest for our souls when we are weary and burdened. His will is for us to live at peace and in joy, which foster good health. The devil is the one who comes to steal, kill, and destroy (John 10:10).

For many years, I was tired most of the time. I didn't sleep well. I had headaches every day, and I struggled with other maladies. But the more my soul was healed, as peace and joy replaced pain in my heart, the healthier I became.

Just as a negative condition of the soul can have a detrimental affect on our body, as our soul becomes stronger and healthier, our body can benefit, too. The apostle John writes about this in 3 John 2: "Dear friend, I pray that you may enjoy good health and that all may go well with you, even as your soul is getting along well" (NIV).

Maybe you have never thought about how much the condition of your soul affects your body, but they are definitely closely connected. As God continues to heal your soul, you can look forward also to improved physical health.

Declare this:

As my soul becomes healthier, I become healthier physically, too.

You Can Have Beauty for Ashes

The Spirit of the Sovereign Lord is on me, because the
Lord has anointed me to proclaim good news to the poor.
He has sent me to... comfort all who mourn, and provide
for those who grieve in Zion—to bestow on them a crown
of beauty instead of ashes.

Isaiah 61:1–3 NIV

Isaiah 61:1–3 has been a life-changing Scripture for me. Part of my personal testimony is that God has given me beauty for ashes, and I know He can do the same for you. This is a powerful promise that I hope will motivate you to continue to follow the Holy Spirit as He brings more and more healing to your soul.

When we think of ashes, we think of something that has been burned up and reduced to an ugly pile of ash that is of no use. When we have been wounded in our soul, the enemy can tempt us to feel that way about who we have become or what our lives have become because of the situations that have hurt or damaged us. But God wants to take the ashes of your past and make something beautiful and new out of them—a beautiful soul and a beautiful life for you.

God's promises are for everyone who knows Him as Father.

The promise of beauty for ashes is a promise for *you*. When people have been wounded in their soul, they sometimes think they are beyond the reach of God's goodness, but that is a lie from the devil. If you know Jesus as your Lord and Savior, every single promise in God's Word applies to your life.

In order to see the promise fulfilled, you will need to give up your ashes. This means you are willing to look ahead and not behind and to stop thinking and talking about the past unless there is a good reason to do so. Giving up your ashes also means believing in faith that, with God's help, your past and all its pain can become nothing more than a memory. I had a very painful childhood, but when I think or talk about it now, it often seems like I am thinking or speaking about someone I once knew a long time ago. The same can happen in your life. That's what a complete work God's healing power can do!

Today is a day to choose to believe that God will make something beautiful out of every place of pain you have ever felt. The beauty God will create in your life will far exceed any kind of beauty you could try to develop in yourself in your own strength. My prayer for you is that God will not only bring you great joy, but that you will also tell others about it so they will be inspired to believe God will give them beauty for their ashes, too.

Declare this:

God is giving me beauty for ashes as He heals my soul.

The Exchange of Righteousness

He made Christ who knew no sin to [judicially] be sin on our behalf, so that in Him we would become the righteousness of God [that is, we would be made acceptable to Him and placed in a right relationship with Him by His gracious lovingkindness].

2 Corinthians 5:21 AMP

Part of being a Christian is being able to exchange all you have for all Jesus has. You can exchange sin for forgiveness, fear for faith, uncertainty for confidence, lack for abundance, anxiety for peace, sadness for joy, despair for hope, failures for a fresh start, weakness for strength, and you can make all kinds of other wonderful exchanges because you belong to God. According to Romans 8:17, believers are "co-heirs with Christ" of all that God gives to Him (NIV). We can have everything He offers us, under one condition: that we give up everything old in order to have the new things He has for us.

I like to say that Jesus invites us to an exchanged life. On any given day with Him, we can make the exchanges I have mentioned in this devotion. But we don't get the new until we release the old.

One of the great exchanges of the Christian life is exchanging our inability to do everything right for the righteousness of God. Isaiah writes that our old righteousness is like filthy rags or a polluted garment (Isa. 64:6), but Jesus' righteousness is perfect. Because of His sacrifice, 2 Corinthians 5:21 tells us that we can exchange our imperfect righteousness for His perfect righteousness.

Have you ever gone through life with a vague sense that something just isn't right about you? You may not be able to articulate it, but you feel it. If you feel that way, I can relate. Because of the abuse that happened during my childhood, I felt for many years that something was wrong with me, but I could never say with certainty what it was. I just knew that for my father to abuse me the way he did, something *had* to be wrong with me. Imagine how thrilled I was when I learned that Jesus makes everything about me right before God through my faith in Him!

The impression that something is wrong about you is a lie from the enemy. The truth is that because of God's lovingkindness, He sees you as right with Him. He accepts you just as you are, holds nothing against you, and helps you become what He wants you to be. You no longer have to carry the burdens of guilt, shame, condemnation, or the feeling that something just isn't right about you. This doesn't mean that every old sense of something being wrong will instantly go away. But it does mean that as you study and meditate on this truth, and as it becomes more and more established in your heart, you will become more and more confident in the fact that your relationship with Jesus has made you completely right with God.

Declare this:

Because of Jesus, I am righteous before God.

85

A Time for Everything

To everything there is a season, a time for every purpose under heaven.

Ecclesiastes 3:1 NKJV

God has His own timing for everything. We know this from Ecclesiastes 3:1 in the Old Testament, and we also know it from 2 Peter 3:8 in the New Testament. Peter writes, "Do not overlook this one fact, beloved, that with the LORD one day is as a thousand years, and a thousand years as one day." When we look at the two verses together, we realize we can be confident that there will be a time for every purpose God has for us, but that timing may not be what we think it should be.

Galatians 6:9 says, "Let us not grow weary of doing good, for in *due season* we will reap, if we do not give up" (italics mine). This verse always seems to encourage people. They seem to be strengthened by simply knowing their good works will eventually reap a harvest. But the verse does not specify *when* they will reap. It only says, "in due season." This is one of several Bible verses that speak of a certain season, rather than a certain year, month, or day. Remember that the Bible even says that only God knows the day and hour when Christ will return (Matt. 24:36). The angels don't know, nor does Jesus Himself. But Scripture does include passages that help us understand the *season* of Christ's return, whether that season is long or short by human standards.

Scriptures that remind us that certain seasons will ultimately come may not offer any insight into the details of God's timing, but they do encourage us to trust Him—and part of spiritual maturity is learning to trust God's timing. We struggle with that until we reach the point that we are surrendered before Him. This means we need to let go of our own agendas, our self-will, our sense of independence, and any effort to "make" things happen in our own strength. When we truly put aside all those things and are ready to let God move *as* He wants to and *when* He wants to, amazing things can happen. Sometimes He is eager to move on our behalf, but restrains Himself because He needs to see that we really do trust Him and are not going to try to take matters into our own hands. His timing is perfect for many reasons, some of which we eventually realize and some we will never know.

Are you trusting God for something in your life? You can rest in the promise of Ecclesiastes 3:1. The season will come for it to manifest for you. If God has purposed it, He will bring it to pass at just the right time, which only He knows. All you have to do is trust Him and enjoy the season you are in.

Declare this:

I trust God's timing completely, knowing that He will fulfill His promises to me in just the right season.

86

Never and Always

Surely I am with you always, to the very end of the age.
Matthew 28:20 NIV

When people teach classes on effective communication, they often advise students to avoid the words *never* and *always.* That's because accusing someone of never doing something or of always being a certain way is rarely accurate. A person may exhibit behaviors or have bad habits most of the time, even 99 percent of the time, but not *always* or *never.*

For example, have you ever heard people arguing and one person accuses another one of never doing their fair share of the work on something? The one accused usually comes back and says, "That is not true..." The words *always* and *never* do not leave room for any exceptions and using them causes us to exaggerate or misrepresent the truth. That's why communication experts say these words have no place in healthy conversation.

God is the only one who can accurately say "never" and "always." His Word is absolute truth, and if He says these words, we can count on them. For example, the Bible says, "The LORD himself goes before you and will be with you; he will *never* leave you nor forsake you. Do not be afraid; do not be discouraged" (Deut. 31:8 NIV, italics mine). God's Word also includes Jesus' promise to remain with us *always* in Matthew 28:20, our verse for today.

The devil often plants thoughts in our minds based on *never* and *always*, because he knows they can entrap us. He tells us the negative aspects of our lives will *never* change and will *always* be the way they are right now. Perhaps he has told you lies such as: "All the women in your family are overweight. You will *never* be slim and trim," or "You don't have the personality to advance at work. You will *always* be stuck in the job you have today," or "You will *always* have to deal with the impact of the abuse in your life. You just can't get over that." These types of thoughts can paralyze you by putting fear in your heart. They can cause you to give up on your dreams and not to even try to pursue God's plans for your life. That's exactly why the enemy gives them to you.

The devil is a liar. Sooner or later, most things change. Negative situations rarely last forever, so our job is to push through them with prayer, patience, and God's help. As we continue to walk in faith, believe God, and trust Him to lead us, we can come out of any negative circumstance in which we find ourselves.

Don't let the enemy ensnare you with thoughts of *never* and *always*. Believe God to change what may *seem* or *feel* like it will never change for you, because the only *never* and *always* that mean anything are the ones in His Word.

Declare this:

I am thankful that God never leaves me, and that I always have hope in Him.

87

Be For Yourself, Not Against Yourself

If God is for us, who can be against us?

Romans 8:31

When we think someone is against is, it's not a good feeling. We want people to be for us, not against us, and to support us rather than try to tear us down. The truth is, there will always be people who are against us, and when that happens, it can be very hurtful. If it happens too much, it can leave a wound in our soul that needs God's healing touch.

I have heard stories from people who felt others were not for them and they still feel that pain of it thirty or forty years later, especially if the person was a parent, a close friend, or a spouse. Sometimes we feel that people are actively working against us, and that brings its own kind of pain. But when we feel that they simply do not care whether we succeed in life or whether we are happy and when they are unwilling to help us, we can feel the pain of being devalued or rejected.

Thankfully, there is one who is always on your side, and that is

God. David writes in Psalm 118:6, "The LORD is on my side; I will not fear." The Lord will fight your battles for you (Exod. 14:14), and He will always lead you to victory (2 Cor. 2:14). He loves you with an everlasting love (Jer. 31:3). He has good plans for your future (Jer. 29:11). He accepts you unconditionally (Eph. 1:6). And according to Psalm 138:8, He *will* fulfill His purpose for your life.

In life, you have to deal with God, with other people, and with yourself. We have established in this devotion that God is for you. In terms of other people, some will be for you and some will be against you. That leaves us with this question: What about you? Are you for or against yourself?

Sometimes when the soul has been wounded, we can become our own worst enemy. We may have listened to other people's judgments against us for so long that we have developed a poor self-image or low self-esteem. We decide we do not like ourselves. We may not appreciate the gifts, talents, and opportunities God has given us. We may feel unworthy of the love of others. We may sabotage ourselves with thoughts that we will never amount to anything. If we think that way, we are likely to end up that way.

One of the most life-changing lessons you can learn is to accept yourself and be for yourself. Becoming your own best friend and ally is one of the best things you can ever do for yourself. I am not talking about being arrogant or insensitive to others, but about believing and agreeing with what God says about you and enjoying who He made you to be.

Declare this:

I am not against myself. Because God is for me, I am, too!

88

Total Forgiveness

*If we confess our sins, he is faithful and just to forgive us
our sins and to cleanse us from all unrighteousness.*

1 John 1:9

In Old Testament times, God's people lived under the Old Covenant, which meant that in order to be forgiven of sin, the person
who sinned had to present an animal sacrifice—a lamb, a calf, a
goat, a turtledove, or a pigeon—to God. Either that person or the
priest laid his hands on the animal's head, confessed the sin, and
acknowledged his guilt. They viewed the animal as a substitute
for the person who had sinned. By putting the animal to death as a
sacrifice, the person covered his sin and could live.

By the time Jesus came to Earth, people understood the
sacrificial system of the Old Covenant well. When John the Bap-
tist referred to Jesus as "the Lamb of God, who takes away the
sin of the world!" (John 1:29), people understood. For generations, their families had sacrificed lambs as substitutes for
their sin.

But now, because of Jesus, we live under the New Covenant.
He became the sacrifice for our sin. Hebrews 9:12 says that He

secured our redemption "not by means of the blood of goats and calves but by means of his own blood."

No matter what you have done, no matter how heavy a burden of shame or guilt you may carry, Jesus' blood has paid for it completely. Because of His sacrifice, God no longer holds that sin against you. You are forgiven. I want to share with you some powerful Scriptures that will help you become established and stand firm in your forgiveness.

- "As far as the east is from the west, so far does he remove our transgressions from us" (Ps. 103:12).
- "In him we have redemption through his blood, the forgiveness of sins, in accordance with the riches of God's grace" (Eph. 1:7 NIV).
- "He has delivered us from the domain of darkness and transferred us to the kingdom of his beloved Son, in whom we have redemption, the forgiveness of sins" (Col. 1:13–14).
- "I will remember their sins and their lawless deeds no more" (Heb. 10:17).
- "Where there is forgiveness of these, there is no longer any offering for sin" (Heb. 10:18).

Part of having your soul healed means receiving the forgiveness God offers you. You may feel you did nothing wrong, nothing to deserve to be hurt, and perhaps you did not. But Romans 3:23 says that "all have sinned and fall short of the glory of God," so that means we *all* need forgiveness. Receiving forgiveness leads to greater freedom.

Declare this:

Because Jesus paid for my sin with His own blood, I am totally forgiven.

How to Handle People
Who Have Hurt You

*But I say to you, Love your enemies and pray for those
who persecute you.*

Matthew 5:44

Dealing with people who have hurt us has gone on throughout
history. Ever since Cain murdered Abel (Gen. 4:8), people have
hurt each other and have had to learn how God wants them to
respond to those who have caused them pain. Our natural instinct
is to want to take revenge and hurt them for hurting us, but that is
not God's will. He forgives us and expects us to forgive others. It
isn't always easy, but if we are willing to obey God, He will give us
the grace to do it.

When we forgive, we are actually doing ourselves a favor by
letting go of thoughts and attitudes that will poison our soul with
bitterness and cause us to be miserable and have no peace.

Even Jesus found that not everyone is trustworthy. His own
disciple, Judas, betrayed Him, and His disciple and close friend,
Peter, denied Him. He also endured other forms of rejection and

pain. He was not a stranger to suffering, yet in Luke 6:27–28, He said, "But I say to you who hear, Love your enemies, do good to those who hate you, bless those who curse you, pray for those who abuse you." When Peter asked Him how often he needed to forgive those who had wronged him, thinking seven times would be enough, Jesus answered, "I do not say to you seven times, but seventy-seven times" (Matt. 18:22), meaning as many times as people need to be forgiven.

The apostle Paul, who had also experienced difficulties in his life, wrote about the importance of "bearing with one another and, if one has a complaint against another, forgiving each other; as the Lord has forgiven you, so you also must forgive" (Col. 3:13).

An important thing to remember is that no one deserves to be treated badly by another person. I didn't deserve to be sexually abused by my father, and you don't deserve the pain or abuse people have caused you. But not deserving to be hurt does not mean we should not forgive and pray for those who have done wrong. In many cases it may not be wise to have personal interaction with those people, but we can pray for them and even help them when they have a need. I did that for my father for many years, and before he died, he received Jesus as his Lord and Savior.

We often find it hard to believe people can change when they have done bad things to us, but all things are possible with God. Always remember that we overcome evil with good (Rom. 12:21).

Declare this:

I choose to forgive and pray for those who have hurt me, and to overcome the evil done to me by being good to others.

All Things Are Possible

*Jesus looked at them and said, "With man it is impossible,
but not with God. For all things are possible with God."*

Mark 10:27

I want to close this devotional with an encouraging word of hope
and victory for you: With God, all things are possible for you.

When we think with our human minds, we can come up with
many reasons certain things may not be possible for us. We may
say, "Good things could never happen for me in the future because
of my past," or "I will never be strong enough or confident enough
to follow my dreams," or "I cannot move beyond the abuse I have
suffered, so I'm not capable of healthy relationships." This kind
of reasoning is rooted in a human way of looking at things. But
God is supernatural. His perspective is totally different than ours,
and He thinks about things in ways we do not. He says through
the prophet Isaiah: "My thoughts are not your thoughts, neither
are your ways my ways, declares the LORD. For as the heavens are
higher than the earth, so are my ways higher than your ways and
my thoughts than your thoughts" (Isa. 55:8–9).

In addition to the fact that God's thoughts are not our thoughts,

I also want to point out that God's abilities are not like our abilities. When our minds tell us we are not able to do something, we tend to believe them. It's true that our human abilities and capacities are limited, and this can cause us to feel frustrated and hopeless. But with God, that never has to happen. When we put our trust in Him, another world opens up to us, a world of possibilities we would have never thought could exist, given our natural abilities. His abilities are unlimited! He has power over everything, and there simply are no obstacles to Him.

The key to living in the possibilities God has for you is to acknowledge that in your own human strength, certain things truly are impossible and to surrender completely to God, trusting Him to do what you cannot. I'm sure there have been times you have tried and tried to accomplish something, and when you finally gave up and turned the situation over to God, you saw Him do with ease what you had struggled with for a long time. I have experienced that many times in my life.

Our continued faith, prayer, and obedience allow us to keep the door open for God to work, so to speak. But if we give up, we may close the door to the miracle He wants to do in our lives.

I urge you to decide today that for the rest of your life, you will keep your mind open to new possibilities. Don't ever allow yourself to think anything is impossible, but stand firm in believing that with God, everything is possible in your life!

Declare this:

With God, all things are possible for me!

Do you have a real relationship with Jesus?

God loves you! He created you to be a special, unique, one-of-a-kind individual, and He has a specific purpose and plan for your life. And through a personal relationship with your Creator—God—you can discover a way of life that will truly satisfy your soul.

No matter who you are, what you've done, or where you are in your life right now, God's love and grace are greater than your sin—your mistakes. Jesus willingly gave His life so you can receive forgiveness from God and have new life in Him. He's just waiting for you to invite Him to be your Savior and Lord.

If you are ready to commit your life to Jesus and follow Him, all you have to do is ask Him to forgive your sins and give you a fresh start in the life you are meant to live. Begin by praying this prayer...

> *Lord Jesus, thank You for giving Your life for me and forgiving me of my sins so I can have a personal relationship with You. I am sincerely sorry for the mistakes I've made, and I know I need You to help me live right.*
>
> *Your Word says in Romans 10:9, "If you declare with your mouth, 'Jesus is Lord,' and believe in your heart that God raised him from the dead, you will be saved" (NIV). I believe You are the Son of God and confess You as my Savior and Lord. Take me just as I am, and work in my heart, making me the person You want me to be. I want to live for You, Jesus, and I am so grateful that You are giving me a fresh start in my new life with You today.*
>
> *I love You, Jesus!*

It's so amazing to know that God loves us so much! He wants to have a deep, intimate relationship with us that grows every day as we spend time with Him in prayer and Bible study. And we want to encourage you in your new life in Christ.

Please visit joycemeyer.org/KnowJesus to request Joyce's book *A New Way of Living*, which is our gift to you. We also have other free resources online to help you make progress in pursuing everything God has for you.

Congratulations on your fresh start in your life in Christ! We hope to hear from you soon.

ABOUT THE AUTHOR

Joyce Meyer is one of the world's leading practical Bible teachers. A *New York Times* bestselling author, Joyce's books have helped millions of people find hope and restoration through Jesus Christ. Joyce's programs, *Enjoying Everyday Life* and *Everyday Answers with Joyce Meyer*, air around the world on television, radio, and the Internet. Through Joyce Meyer Ministries, Joyce teaches internationally on a number of topics with a particular focus on how the Word of God applies to our everyday lives. Her candid communication style allows her to share openly and practically about her experiences so others can apply what she has learned to their lives.

Joyce has authored more than 100 books, which have been translated into more than 100 languages, and over 65 million of her books have been distributed worldwide. Bestsellers include *Power Thoughts*; *The Confident Woman*; *Look Great, Feel Great*; *Starting Your Day Right*; *Ending Your Day Right*; *Approval Addiction*; *How to Hear from God*; *Beauty for Ashes*; and *Battlefield of the Mind*.

Joyce's passion to help hurting people is foundational to the vision of Hand of Hope, the missions arm of Joyce Meyer Ministries. Hand of Hope provides worldwide humanitarian outreaches such as feeding programs, medical care, orphanages, disaster response, human trafficking intervention and rehabilitation, and much more—always sharing the love and Gospel of Christ.

JOYCE MEYER MINISTRIES U.S. & FOREIGN OFFICE ADDRESSES

Joyce Meyer Ministries
P.O. Box 655
Fenton, MO 63026
USA
(636) 349-0303

Joyce Meyer Ministries—Canada
P.O. Box 7700
Vancouver, BC V6B 4E2
Canada
(800) 868-1002

Joyce Meyer Ministries—Australia
Locked Bag 77
Mansfield Delivery Centre
Queensland 4122
Australia
(07) 3349 1200

Joyce Meyer Ministries—England
P.O. Box 1549
Windsor SL4 1GT
United Kingdom
01753 831102

Joyce Meyer Ministries—South Africa
P.O. Box 5
Cape Town 8000
South Africa
(27) 21-701-1056

OTHER BOOKS BY JOYCE MEYER

Seven Things That Steal Your Joy
Start Your New Life Today
Starting Your Day Right
Straight Talk
Teenagers Are People Too!
Trusting God Day by Day
The Word, the Name, the Blood
Woman to Woman
You Can Begin Again
Your Battles Belong to the Lord*

JOYCE MEYER SPANISH TITLES

Belleza en Lugar de Cenizas (Beauty for Ashes)
Buena Salud, Buena Vida (Good Health, Good Life)
Cambia Tus Palabras, Cambia Tu Vida
(Change Your Words, Change Your Life)
El Campo de Batalla de la Mente (Battlefield of the Mind)
Como Formar Buenos Habitos y Romper Malos Habitos
(Making Good Habits, Breaking Bad Habits)
La Conexión de la Mente (The Mind Connection)
Dios No Está Enojado Contigo (God Is Not Mad at You)
La Dosis de Aprobación (The Approval Fix)
Efesios: Comentario Biblico (Ephesians: Biblical Commentary)
Empezando Tu Día Bien (Starting Your Day Right)
Hazte un Favor a Ti Mismo…Perdona (Do Yourself a Favor…Forgive)
Madre Segura de Sí Misma (The Confident Mom)
Pensamientos de Poder (Power Thoughts)
Sanidad para el Alma de una Mujer (Healing the Soul of a Woman)
Santiago: Comentario Bíblico (James: Biblical Commentary)
Sobrecarga (Overload)*
Sus Batallas Son del Señor (Your Battles Belong to the Lord)

Termina Bien Tu Día (Ending Your Day Right)
Usted Puede Comenzar de Nuevo (You Can Begin Again)
Viva Valientemente (Living Courageously)

*Study Guide available for this title

BOOKS BY DAVE MEYER

Life Lines